Ceramics
of the '50s & '60s

A Collector's Guide

Ceramics
of the '50s & '60s

A Collector's Guide

Steven Jenkins

MILLER'S CERAMICS OF THE '50S & '60S: A COLLECTOR'S GUIDE
by Steven Jenkins

First published in Great Britain in 2001 by Miller's, a division of
Mitchell Beazley, imprints of Octopus Publishing Group Ltd,
2–4 Heron Quays, London E14 4JP

Miller's is a registered trademark of Octopus Publishing Group Ltd

Copyright © Octopus Publishing Group Ltd 2001

Commissioning Editor **Anna Sanderson**
Deputy Art Director **Vivienne Brar**
Senior Art Editor **Rhonda Fisher**
Project Editor **Emily Anderson**
Designer **Louise Griffiths**
Editor **Claire Musters**
Proofreader **Laura Hicks**
Indexer **Sue Farr**
Picture Research **Jenny Faithfull, Nick Wheldon**
Production **Catherine Lay**
Jacket photography by **Steve Tanner**

The publishers will be grateful for any information that will assist them
in keeping future editions up to date. Although all reasonable care
has been taken in the preparation of this book, neither the publishers
nor the compilers can accept any liability for any consequence arising
from the use thereof, or the information contained therein.

ISBN 1 84000 372 3
A CIP catalogue record for this book is available from the British Library
Set in Bembo, Frutiger and Shannon
Produced by Toppan Printing Co., (HK) Ltd.
Printed and bound in China

Jacket illustrations, clockwise from top left: Jessie Tait Midwinter vase,
c.1956, £250–300/$400–480; Homemaker plate, c.1955, £12–15/$20–25;
Italian ashtray, c.1960, £5–8/$8–13; Portmeirion Monte Sol storage jar,
1965, £18–22/$30–35; **back cover:** Woods & Sons "Hedgerow" milk jug,
1950s, £8–10/$13–16; **half-title page:** Swinnertons plate, 1950s, £20–25/
$32–40; **contents page:** Wade cup and saucer, 1950s, £18–22/$30–35

contents

Introduction

In Britain up until 1952 there was little to buy in the way of ceramics, and any pieces that were available were either undecorated or "seconds"; all the better-quality decorated ware was exported to boost the country's income after World War II. Many potteries had been requisitioned for war work and needed a great deal of effort to take them back up to their pre-war standard. Scandinavian countries continued production throughout the 1940s and were quite advanced in design terms. The USA and Canada had also continued to produce pottery, and many emigrants from Europe had started businesses or were designing for prominent companies in the USA. Much of what we think of as "classic" 1950s design is American. Britain caught on to the new trends from about 1952.

Images used on pottery often filtered down from modern art, which influenced textile

Pair of "Piazza-ware" vases by Woods (see pp.22-3), late 1950s, ht 20cm/8in, **£35–50/$55–80**

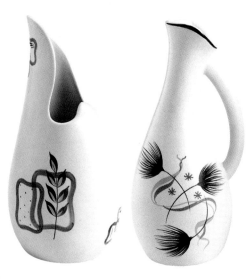

designers, who produced progressive patterns that were adapted for dinner or tea ware. The British public, who had been starved of new decorative ceramics after the war, made it clear that they wanted freedom of choice and something "contemporary". The Festival of Britain in 1951 gave them just this (see pp.8–9).

In the USA, in the late 1930s, Russel Wright designed tableware with organic and freeform shapes. Aptly named "American Modern", these pieces were sold in the 1950s along with Eva Zeisel's dinnerware designs for Redwing and Hall China. In Sweden, Stig Lindberg was a prolific ceramic designer.

The influence of art and technology was plain to see on the ceramics of the 1950s. Dali and Miró motifs turned up on all sorts of ware, as did sputniks and stars. Polka dots, checks or plaids and zebra stripes moved from fashionable dresses to tableware. Colours were fresh and bright – yellow, scarlet and lime green were popular and often mixed with stark but stylish black and white. Neapolitan sets, in which a series of colours could be mixed and matched, broke the formality of table settings.

As the 1960s began, the fluid shapes of the past decade were becoming predictable, so geometric and cylindrical shapes emerged. Colours became subtle or deeper, with more natural tones. However, pop art and fashion once again showed their influence as "flower power" and psychedelia took over on some designs. On the less fashionable, mainstream side of production a retrogressive move towards naturalistic and traditional motifs on "antique" shapes was a reaction against the exuberance of the previous decade. Technology had also progressed, and hand painting all but disappeared from the larger factories, although some still managed to create a "hand-painted look" that fitted the times perfectly.

Lemonade set by Thomas, Germany, 1960s,
ht 30cm/12in, **£40–50/$65–80**

Where to start

If you are just starting your collection of 1950s
and 1960s ware, the companies that produced
only decorative ware, as opposed to tea and
dinnerware, are easier to begin with. Scout
around and don't be afraid of car-boot and
garage sales – there are still some lucky finds
out there. Local antiques fairs and flea markets
can be good hunting grounds, but there are
also specialist 20thC fairs now, as well as small
shops dealing in "retro culture", where you are
more likely to find a large selection of pieces.
Prices tend to be higher at these places,
but you will gain the convenience of choice.

An advertisement in a local newspaper's
classifieds can also turn up items, and there
are collectors' magazines to look out for too.
    Be realistic when you decide what you are
collecting – it may take you years to amass a
collection, as finding pieces does take time.
And if you do see a piece that you have been
looking for, but it is more expensive than you
had hoped, or there is minor damage, think
twice before you walk away. Every collector
has stories of "the piece I left behind". You
could take the telephone number of the seller,
or see if the dealer will be at the same venue
next time. This forethought can save a lot of
heartache later on. Whatever you decide to
collect, the 1950s and 1960s were full of fun
and innovative designs, so enjoy yourself.

Prices & dimensions

Prices vary, depending on the condition of the
item, its rarity and where it is purchased, so
the prices given are an approximate guide only.
The sterling/dollar conversion has been made
at a rate of £1 = $1.60 (adjust the dollar value as
necessary to accord with current exchange rates).
Size is to the nearest half centimetre/quarter
inch; ht, diam., w. and l. abbreviations are used.

Wedgwood & Festival of Britain

Wedgwood commissioned some of the most prominent artists of the day to design for the company. In 1951 a series of exhibitions and displays was organized throughout Great Britain, known as the Festival of Britain, and Wedgwood produced display items as well as souvenirs for the Festival. New designs, exciting scientific developments and modern architecture were shown there alongside Britain's history. A huge number of painters, sculptors and designers produced work – everything in the exhibition was specially commissioned and designed in the new "contemporary" style. Young people liked the vision of the future and wanted this look for their own homes. Although it took some years to filter into shops, the exuberance and colour of the Festival of Britain set the style for the next decade.

Festival of Britain mug by Norman Makison, 1951, ht 7cm/2¾in, **£200–250/ $320–400**

◀ **Festival of Britain mug by Norman Makison**
This souvenir item from the Festival features the Crystal Palace, site of the Great Exhibition of 1851 (whose 100th anniversary was celebrated during the Festival), and the Skylon and Dome of Discovery from 1951. Hand painting in red and blue adds a patriotic touch to the small mug, which is only 7cm (2¾in) high. The Festival's logo can be seen clearly on the mug's base. As one of the expensive ceramic souvenirs of London's South Bank Exhibition, which was only open from May to September 1951, this item is now very scarce and highly collectable.

▼ **Coronation mug by Eric Ravilious**
Although Eric Ravilious had been killed during World War II, many of his pottery designs for Wedgwood were not produced until much later, during the 1950s. This Coronation mug was adapted from his 1936 design for Edward VIII's coronation: the colours were changed and the numerals adapted to read 1953. The fireworks that can be seen on this mug were to become a popular post-war image, symbolizing celebration. Produced in much larger quantities than the smaller festival mug, this is still a highly sought-after item.

Coronation mug by Eric Ravilious, 1953, ht 12cm/4¾in, **£150–200/ $240–320**

There is an enormous selection of souvenirs from the Festival, but few are as tasteful as the Wedgwood mug. Many factories just added lettering to existing designs or used poor-quality motifs on "seconds". However, all of these pieces still have their place in the social history of the day.

"Garden" plates by Eric Ravilious, 1950s, diam. 21cm/8¼in and 26cm/10¼in, **£300–400/$480–640**

▲ "Garden" plates by Eric Ravilious

The "Garden" pattern featured a wealth of illustrations. Each size of plate has a different central image, but all are unified with a common border, most often a graduated yellow band (the blue band is much more unusual). Small items like coffee cans and teacups just incorporate the border design and are therefore cheaper – unusual items, like the meat plate featuring a swimming pool, are likely to be the most expensive of the range.

▼ "Persephone" oval bowl by Eric Ravilious

This is probably the easiest Ravilious pattern to find, and, confusingly, it is sometimes backstamped Harvest Festival. It is also found in black on white (which may be of seconds quality and sold at a lower price) as well as in various coloured bandings. The same illustration of fish and cornucopias is used throughout the service. This particular piece is a great example of Ravilious' work and so is very collectable.

"Persephone" oval bowl by Eric Ravilious, 1950s, diam. 25cm/10in, **£300–400/$480–640**

"Zodiac Bull", 1946, l. 40cm/16in, **£300–350/$480–560**

▲ "Zodiac Bull"

This sculptural figure is thought to be one of the first new designs produced in Britain after the war. Modelled by Arnold Machin, the "Zodiac Bull" superseded "Ferdinand", a florally decorated model made for export. The Zodiac Bull was sold in Britain in the 1950s; it was the quintessential ornament of its day. The Wedgwood mark and date of manufacture are impressed into the underside of the body in place of the usual transfer, which may have been too visible on this design.

The pattern and artist names are found at the top of these stamps, often with a Wedgwood mark and date too.

GARDEN
DESIGNED BY
RAVILIOUS
OF ETRURIA
WEDGWOOD
MADE IN
ENGLAND
BARLASTON

American 1950s

The USA was ahead of Britain in design terms in the early 1950s; the geometric, harsh lines of 1930s pottery had developed into fluid, organic shapes under the influence of painters like Salvador Dali and Joan Mirò. New styles of decoration had also filtered through from fine art and sculpture. Ceramics were of softer shades, in a selection of pastel and natural colours. Speckled glazes toned in with interior "barkcloth" fabrics, and stars, sputniks and amoebic shapes were used as decoration. Because of the size of the USA a huge variety of wares was created, in all price brackets, and much of it is still circulating in good condition today. Designer names are obviously worth more, but there is a wealth of great designs from smaller and lesser-known factories too. For example, figural lamp bases from the 1950s have great appeal and can help create a period look.

▼ **Grey jug and yellow bowl by Russel Wright**
Russel Wright (1904–76) had a huge influence on ceramic design. His "Casual China", which has a softness as though it is melting, was popular in the 1950s. The sculptural quality here makes the items as decorative as they are functional. The speckles in the glaze colours and the mix-and-match palette are both typical of the period.

Russel Wright grey jug, ht 33cm/13in, **£50–60/ $80–95;** yellow bowl, diam. 28cm/ 11in, **£25–35/ $40–55**

▲ **"Town and Country" individual covered dishes by Eva Zeisel**
Eva Zeisel embraced the modern organic look after the war, and her "Town and Country" dinnerware design for Redwing Pottery in 1946 was daring and innovative, influencing the work of many potteries in the 1950s. Bright, clean colours and imaginative forms are her trademark – the use of an integral handle on items was groundbreaking.

"Town and Country" dishes by Eva Zeisel, 1946, diam. c.18cm/7in (from edge to end of handle of both), **£30–40/ $50–65 (each)**

It is best to focus on a look or a factory when starting a collection from the USA as there is so much to choose from. The work of one designer can be a fun and challenging area to begin with. Collecting for investment may mean you pay more than the current market price now, but a piece in demand will accumulate in value.

FACT FILE

▼ **"Fiesta" ware by Frederick Hurten Rhead**
This colourful everyday tableware is a quintessential example of American 1950s design. Available in a range of bright colours to mix and match, some pieces are still in production today, and most bear the "Fiesta" name on the base. The ridged border on flatware items is mirrored by concentric circles on serving items. Collectors should be wary of modern versions, which are much lighter than the originals.

"Fiesta" ware by Frederick Hurten Rhead, 1950s, jug, ht 19cm/7½in, **£75–100/$120–160;** covered dish, diam. 21.5cm/8½in, **£30–40/$50–65**

Cat cruet by Holt Howard, late 1950s, ht 11cm/4¼in, **£25–30/$40–50**

▲ **Cat cruet by Holt Howard**
This delightful duo originally had sound effects when shaken. Sadly these no longer work, but the original Holt Howard tag remains intact. Cats and poodles were popular motifs throughout the 1950s, and these items were made in Japan for the US market. Many Holt Howard pieces are dated on the bases and have "HH" marks. The pottery is prone to chipping and flaking, so beware of repair and restoration. The "cute" factor ensures that the prices paid for these pieces will continue to rise.

"Jam 'n jelly" figural pot, late 1950s, ht 9cm/3½in, **£18–22/$30–35**

▲ **"Jam 'n jelly" figural pot**
This decorative pot was made in Japan for the US market. The appealing face actually has a dual purpose as it is also the lid; the base of the lid doubles as a spoon so that honey, mustard or jam can be served easily. Unfortunately the spoons are very fragile, and the damage quotient is quite high. You can expect to find a little damage on most of these pieces, and will have to pay a premium for any in pristine condition.

T. G. Green & Co. Ltd.

The English pottery T. G. Green & Co. Ltd. is best known for its striped "Cornish ware" design, which dates back to the 1920s. This was the kitchen accessory that every household in the 1950s had to have, and the blue-and-white version is still popular today. Banding and clean graphic lines were the trademark designs of this factory, but stencil designs were also used extensively. Some of Green's 1950s and 1960s designs are surprisingly fashion-conscious: it actually produced a TV-screen-shaped dinner plate in the early 1950s. Its gingham, striped and spotted patterns are now classics, but interest in the modern-styled patterns is increasing. The "Gayday" range, which was advertised in 1960, moved on to the simpler look of the new decade, using strong geometric shapes to form repeat patterns.

"Cornish" mixing bowl and smaller bowl, 1950s, mixing bowl diam. 23.5cm/9¼in, **£20–30/$30–50**; smaller bowl diam. 16cm/6¼in, **£18–22/$30–35**

▲ "Cornish" mixing bowl and smaller bowl

No self-respecting 1950s housewife would have been without some blue-and-white kitchenware. Most items were highly functional, and the mixing bowl was designed to sit comfortably at an angle for ease of use. On authentic T. G. Green pieces the blue areas of the striped pattern are always in relief and the white areas recessed. The updated back-stamp has a church or a shield alongside the company name (see opposite page).

▼ "Blue Domino" ware

Here is the classic blue and white combination again, this time with polka dots. These should feel as though they are impressed into the clay, as they are made by paper dots being applied to the plate and the blue slip sprayed over the top. The dots are peeled off, and the plate is then ready to be glazed. This was a good mix-and-match pattern to the striped Cornish ware and it, too, still has pieces in production today. The larger jug was a trial piece and was not available to buy.

"Blue Domino" ware, 1950s, large jug ht 28cm /11in; gravy boat w. 18cm/7in, **£30–40/$50–65**; small jug w. 9cm/3½in, **£18–22/$30–35**

"Fleur" casserole and plate, early 1960s, casserole diam. 21.5cm/8½in, **£30–35/$50–55**; plate diam. 25.5cm/10in, **£12–15/$20–25**

▲ **"Fleur" casserole and plate**
This Scandinavian-inspired pattern features wonderful floral and herbal images that are reminiscent of Marianne Westman's "Picknick" for Rorstrand (see p.26). In this design the border pattern is formed by simple black prints that are then hand coloured. A rich dark-green glaze is used on the lids and hollow-ware accessories. The pattern was relatively popular when it was made, but it was actually only available for a short time in the early 1960s.

▼ **"Central Park" plate**
This pattern is part of a range in the fashionable "Patio Modern" shape. It is based on square forms, and there are square button knobs on the pots, and softened square cups and jugs. This shows the influence of Eva Zeisel and the American "new look" on British ceramics. Other patterns in the range included "Samba" and "Safari". "Central Park" is a transfer pattern that has naturalistic and stylized leaf patterns in a row across flatware, and a soft rust-coloured glaze inside the cups and on the lids. It is a good example of the fact that the bright palette of the early 1950s was already toning down to more natural shades by 1957.

"Central Park" plate, 1957, diam. 28cm/11in, **£24–28/$40–45**

"Roulette" teacup, saucer and side plate, early 1960s, side plate diam. 18cm/7in, **£25–30/$40–50 (for the set)**

▲ **"Roulette" teacup, saucer and side plate**
This pattern probably dates from the early 1960s, and has here been put on the "Gayday" range of shapes. These were more streamlined than the "Patio Modern" shape; the casserole or vegetable dishes had no side handles, and looked "space age", but the plates had returned to a traditional shape. The design was applied through a stencil.

Wade

The Wade factory produced some of its most graphic pieces of pottery during the 1950s. Many of these are easily recognized by their strong use of colour – stark black and white, bright red and strong yellow. These, combined with the fashionable images and fluid shapes, make Wade one of the best factories to collect for an authentic 1950s look. However, despite such a loyal commitment to modern design, the factory, like many others, produced a large percentage of traditional ware, as the "contemporary" market was felt to be unstable. Ashtrays, fruit bowls and decorative items were produced with up-to-the-minute imagery, but more mainstream images of harvesting or London scenes broadened the sales potential. In the 1960s animal figures took over, and there was less fashion-driven design apparent in the factory output.

"Zamba" black-and-white vase, late 1950s, ht 25cm/10in, **£35–45/$55–70**

▶ **"Zamba" black-and-white vase**
The "Zamba" range was used on many different shapes, and the bold decorations in black and white make these great items to collect. Lively tribal dancers bound all over the equally lively shapes, which include ashtrays, small jugs and extravagantly shaped vases. Unfortunately, the unusual shapes are prone to hairline cracks, and the black enamel on the inside is liable to craze and eventually peel. Look out for repainting inside these vases as very often it is not sympathetically worked and can detract from an otherwise very attractive item.

▼ **Illustrated trays by Rowland Emmet**
Rowland Emmet was a well-known illustrator of the day. His gentle humour and typically English eccentricity meant his work appealed to most people. These trays are tinted with popular pastel shades. They could be used as coasters, ashtrays or nut dishes and would have made an ideal gift item at the time.

Trays by Rowland Emmet, late 1950s, w. 11cm/4¼in, **£8–12/$13–20**

Figural cat vases, late 1950s, ht 11.5cm/4½in, **£50–60/$80–95**

▲ Figural cat vases

This pair of cat vases is typical of the Wade style of the late 1950s – strong and highly graphic. The interior of the vases is finished with an on-glaze red enamel, and this can discolour or flake off with age. The four-prong feet are typical of 1950s style – most fashion-conscious factories produced footed or pronged shapes to echo the spindle-legged furniture in vogue at the time. As this fashion was superseded these ornaments would have looked dated, and many may have been thrown away.

▼ "Shooting star" jug

This jug is part of the "Harmony" range. Fruit bowls on feet, hourglass vases and items with rows of "portholes" were among the most popular shapes. Also available in simple colour combinations of grey and pink, or black and lime green, these were often sold without decoration to let the shapes speak for themselves. The shooting star motif was used on these shapes with a glossy black interior. The pink and yellow of the design was intended to have been picked out in the wallpaper or fabric of the room in which it was placed.

"Shooting star" jug, late 1950s, ht 9cm/3½in, **£40–45/$65–70**

▼ "Parasols" fruit bowl

This is another example of the "Harmony" range of shapes. It demonstrates the daring use of holes in contemporary design, which may have filtered down from the sculptural work of Henry Moore and his contemporaries. These transfer-printed parasols on white shapes were a light-hearted motif suggestive of French fashion, interest in which had revived during that period. Less popular than the "Shooting Star" pattern at the time, "Parasols" is now not so easy to find and is thus more desirable to today's collector.

"Parasols" fruit bowl, late 1950s, ht 18.5cm/7¼in, **£60–70/$95–110**

W a d e ~ 15

Colin Melbourne

Although Colin Melbourne (*b.* 1928) is not really a familiar name to many collectors he did in fact work for many of the larger factories during the 1950s, and was also in partnership with the designer David Queensberry during the 1960s. Using a strong sculptural element in his work, Melbourne produced many figural items of great quality and distinction for the Beswick and Midwinter potteries. His other work for both factories included a small range of vases for Midwinter and a huge selection of shapes and decorations for Beswick. His work was very modern and perhaps a little too ahead of its time for the general public of the day, but the breadth of work that he produced shows his real commitment to modern design. His collaboration with Crown Devon resulted in the classic "Memphis" range, which today is probably the most recognized range produced by Melbourne.

▼ **Cat figure for Midwinter**
Colin Melbourne was asked to design some contemporary ornaments and figures for Midwinter in about 1956, and this resulted in a strange mixture of, among others, dinosaurs, giraffes and cats. The figures often have delicate features and are prone to damage. Many are not back-stamped and can only be recognized by the shape numbers on the bases of the figures. The relative rarity of these figures ensures that they will always be sought after.

Cat figure for Midwinter, c.1956, w. 24cm/9½in, **£125–175/ $200–280**

▶ **Green vase for Beswick**
Following the success of Colin Melbourne's designs for Midwinter, Beswick added to their range of "modern" designs by asking Melbourne to create a series of extremely advanced decorative items. A back-stamp with his facsimile signature was used on this ware. Coloured glazes and sgrafitto (see p.60) decorated these already progressive and organic shapes. Leaf forms and abstract circular patterns were drawn onto the body of the pieces, so that each one of them became an original, sculptural piece of pottery – aimed at the more expensive end of the market.

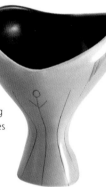

Green vase for Beswick, c.1956, ht 14.5cm/5¾in, **£80–100/ $130–160**

Orange/brown animal vase for Beswick, c.1956, ht 19.5cm/7¾in, **£150–200/$240–320**

▲ Orange/brown animal vase for Beswick

This vase shows how extreme were the shapes that Melbourne created for the Beswick factory. The simple, organic decoration adds to the primitive look here. Owing to their daring shapes such vases are not likely to have survived intact in large quantities, which makes them well worth finding.

▼ "Memphis" vase for Crown Devon

This is one of the most graphic and commercial pieces of Colin Melbourne's work from the early 1960s. "Memphis", as the name suggests, seems to have been inspired by temples and monuments in ancient Egypt. Bright-gold chevron designs accentuate the decorative black, white or, much rarer, turquoise glaze-coloured items. There is a wide variety of vase shapes – from posy holders through to elegant vases. None of them is inexpensive, but they are always popular with collectors.

"Memphis" vase for Crown Devon, early 1960s, ht 18cm/7in, **£40–60/$65–95**

• There are pieces of the Beswick "CM" range finished in plain white or single-glaze colours. These do not command the prices of decorated items and do not carry Melbourne's signature.
• Some Melbourne-style bowls from the 1950s have a Midwinter stamp. They may have been inspired by Melbourne's work, but he is not credited with their design.

▼ "Petra" vase for Royal Norfolk

This highly artistic range, designed in the 1960s, shows few of the influences that were at play during the 1950s. Highly abstract screen-printed transfers are combined here with terracotta relief on a glazed white body. Each of the shapes in the range has a unique panel of texture. The vase shown below has fern leaves in relief on the unglazed area, possibly indicating that the inspiration for the whole range was from fossils and strata.

"Petra" vase for Royal Norfolk, 1960s, ht 29cm/11½in, **£30–40/ $50–65**

There is no mistaking the bold title and facsimile signature below. Many Beswick pieces simply have a "CM" stamp, while Midwinter animals generally have no mark on them at all.

Colin Melbourne ~ 17

Beswick

John Beswick founded his company in the late 1920s, and from the outset he always had an eye for fashion. After World War II, as more and more potteries slowly stepped into the fashion market for ceramics, the Beswick factory made a bold move with its extremely daring range of decorative vases and bowls designed by Albert Hallam. Colin Melbourne added to this modern look by producing an "Art" range in 1956 for the factory (see pp.16–17). Conscious of the impact that Midwinter was making with its abstract designs on square-shaped tableware, Beswick produced its own version, using modern handles on fashionably shaped wares. The use of illustrative transfer patterns continued through into the 1960s, and these whimsical images have become quintessential examples of post-war British tableware design.

◀ **"Circus" teapot**
This pattern has become one of the most collected of the 1950s Beswick tableware patterns. The simplicity of the figures and the flat colour make this a very graphic pattern. "Circus" was produced on a wide range of functional items, such as jam pots and butter dishes. Cups and saucers are fairly easy to find, but the tea and coffee pots are the real collectors' pieces of the range. Teapots usually fetch a premium over coffee-pots as they would have been in general use (unlike the coffee-pots, which tended to be cabinet pieces), so pristine teapots are highly sought after.

"Circus" teapot, 1950s, ht 14cm/5½in, **£90–120/ $145–190**

▼ **"Ballet" plate**
Ballet dancers and related images were pictured on everything in the 1950s – brooches, headscarves, prints and all manner of pottery. This design, referred to as both "Pavlova" and "Ballet" on its backstamps, is one of the most popular and easily found patterns in this theme. Cups and the bases of jam and butter dishes were worked in turquoise glaze, and the insides of cups showed a couple caught mid-dance. This has become one of the most popular illustrated patterns, not only of Beswick's but of the 1950s, and was probably produced into the 1960s as well.

"Ballet" plate, 1950s–1960s, diam. 25cm/10in, **£15–25/ $25–40**

Zebra-striped ware, 1950s, left:
"Zebrette" vase ht 20cm/8in, £25–
30/$40–50; right: Beswick vase
ht 12cm/4¾in, £45–55/$70–90

▲ Zebra-striped ware

The Beswick zebra-striped
range was the most popular
and prominent of a number
of patterns used to decorate
these wares. Inspired by Jessie
Tait's "Zambesi" pattern,
produced for Midwinter, Albert
Hallam's wild organic shapes
made a big impact on 1950s
pottery. Bold black stripes were
painted on the outside, and
bright yellow or red on-glaze
enamels were applied to
the interiors, giving a
striking finish to the pieces.
The "Zebrette" vase on
the left was produced
by Sandland Ware.
Although the shapes
are different there is
little difference in the
execution or collectability
of the two, and most
collectors are happy to mix.

▼ "Dawn Chorus" jug

The "Dawn Chorus" pattern
evokes the optimistic feel of
the 1950s with its positive,
bright image of lively birds
drawn in a loose style. Seen
less often than other patterns
in the series, it is nevertheless
still charming. Other patterns
include "Happy Morn", which
can be found on the same
shape and has vignettes of a
couple on their wedding day,
and "Dancing Days", which
pictures a barrel organ, organ
grinder and monkey alternating
with a dancing couple. A
collection of these different
patterns can look great together.

"Dawn Chorus" jug, 1950s, ht
13cm/5in, £18–22/$30–35

Alfred Meakin

Alfred Meakin produced a wealth of affordable dinnerware throughout the 1950s, and although many of the patterns were supplied "open stock", and were therefore available to a number of factories, Meakin did produce some unique patterns for those setting up home for the first time. Among the traditional floral patterns and rose bouquets are some patterns with lively cacti and everyday scenes, which were often light-hearted and cartoon-like in style. Inspired by films, the factory produced patterns like "My Fair Lady" and "The Gay Nineties" (the latter featuring suited gentlemen on precarious bicycles and ladies in wasp-waisted dresses with parasols). Although collected by those trying to re-create 1950s interiors in their homes today, the Meakin product has not yet become a mainstream collectable, but this is sure to change in the next few years. The hand-painted ranges in the Midwinter style, with checks or plaids, spots and stripes, are worth looking out for.

▼ **"Jivers" jug and sugar bowl**

This jug and sugar bowl are typical of the mix of contemporary decoration and traditional shape that many British factories adopted during the 1950s. The stylized dancers in primary red and yellow date from about 1958. This is one of the hardest Meakin patterns to find. Today "Jivers" pieces are keenly collected by those interested in the rock-and-roll scene and other 1950s revivals.

"Jivers" jug and sugar bowl, c.1958, jug ht 10cm/4in, bowl diam. 11.5cm/4½in, **£28–35/ $45–55 (the pair)**

▶ **"Seine" coffee-pot**

This coffee-pot is a superb example of its style – the image covers a large area and it still has its platinum lustre banding intact on the lid, handle and rim. Foreign travel became easier towards the end of the 1950s, and this was reflected in the decorations on pottery and fabrics. The lid on this pot shows small café scenes. Paris was thought to be the centre of style and fashion, and the Parisian lady with her poodle was the epitome of French culture. A riverside scene on the back of the pot adds ambience to the design.

"Seine" coffee-pot, late 1950s, ht 18cm/7in, **£45–50/ $70–80**

▼ Café and fairground plates

This colourful series on traditionally shaped earthenware was aimed at the mainstream market, intended for everyday use. Because they were not "best" tableware they were made in large quantities and heavily used. This means that the condition of surviving items can be poor. The on-glaze transfers suffer from knife marks, and sometimes they and the gold lustre rim bands have all but worn away. However, this should not affect the overall value.

Café and fairground plates, 1950s, diam. 17cm/6¾in, **£8–20/$13–32 (each)**

"Bill and Ben" plate and green cup with saucer, early 1960s, plate diam. 17cm/6¾in, **£20–25/$32–40 (the set)**

▲ "Bill and Ben" plate and green cup with saucer

Television was starting to play a larger part in people's lives during the 1950s. Children's television was creative and fun, and this pattern from the early 1960s is named after a popular British puppet programme, where the central characters lived in flower pots. As a slight change from the ware of the 1950s, teacups were made of a single glaze colour. A similar pattern with cacti is just one other example of these exciting 1960s transfer patterns, which are great fun to collect today.

• Meakin patterns have not become widely popular with collectors in the same way that both Midwinter and Homemaker have, as they were not produced in quite the same quantities. The limited range of shapes can be frustrating for the collector, but the variety of decorative patterns should make up for that.

• Following on from the popularity of "Western" films, a series of patterns on the cowboy theme was produced. Some are graphic, with wagons and horses in silhouette, but others are in full colour and have all the appeal of the "Jivers" or "Seaside" patterns.

This basic generic backstamp is found on most of the 1950s and early 1960s Meakin tableware. Occasionally a pattern would also have a small image and title for use with the backstamp (for example, many of the nautical patterns).

Woods

Woods embraced the trends of the post-war period with both decorative and functional ranges and was best known for its single-colour services, used in hospitals, cafés and homes across the country; the "Berol", "Jasmine" and "Iris" ranges were some of the best utilitarian designs and are still in production today. The "Ringwood" shape was a development of these, but it made a conscious effort to keep up-to-date without overstepping the mark. Probably intended to appeal to the export market, which was potentially much larger than the UK market, some patterns on "Ringwood" ware seem quite uncharacteristic of Woods. In contrast to the dinnerware is the decorative "Piazza" ware, which was the height of fashion in its day. Decorated by hand on matt white glazes with bright colours, on a broad range of organic sculptural shapes, these were well-designed pieces aimed at the masses.

"Hedgerow" teapot, 1950s, ht 13cm/5in, £25–30/ $40–50

◀ **"Hedgerow" teapot**
This small "tea-for-two" teapot shows the best features of the "Ringwood" shape. The ridges at the top of the pot strengthen the shape, while the general lines make it as if it is leaning forwards, which was a welcome change from the static look of the more traditional shapes of the day. The decoration is a stylized natural pattern printed in brown and hand-coloured; there are many other different colour versions to be found.

▼ **Polka-dot cup and saucer**
This cup and saucer have the trademark "Ringwood" ridges, which are both decorative and practical, on the edge of the saucer and the base of the cup. The dot pattern is from a printed transfer, and the red details were added on after-wards by hand. As the red is an underglaze it is not as bright as the on-glaze enamels that were used by other factories. This pattern would have been aimed at the younger buyer, as polka dots were considered the height of fashionable good taste during the 1950s.

Polka-dot cup and saucer, saucer diam. 15cm/6in, cup ht 7cm/2¾in, £10–15/ $15–25

Transfers were made to look like hand painting, so extra scrutiny is required to ensure that the pieces you are looking at are in fact hand-painted. Comparison of the same two items should solve this problem, as no two hand-painted pieces will be identical.

"Carnival" jug and sugar bowl, 1950s, jug ht 9cm/3½in, bowl ht 5.5cm/2¼in, **£25–30/$40–50 (the pair)**

▲ **"Carnival" jug and sugar bowl**
This pattern was likely to have been intended for the export market as today it turns up mostly in Canada. The repeat pattern suited the shapes – especially the "TV" cup and plate sets. The print is dark grey, hand-coloured in yellow. A half tone on the design dispenses with the need for an additional colour, making the pattern easy and not too expensive to produce. Large quantities of these patterns would have been made, but as they were intended for everyday use condition can be poor on the surviving items.

▼ **"Piazza-ware" vase**
This range of vases, ashtrays and even a toastrack used both abstract and figurative designs. The shapes are fluid as the clay was forced into the most extravagant shapes, following the style of contemporary American designers. The matt finish was typical of "fancy" wares of the late 1950s and early 1960s, and this gave the items a hand-crafted look, which was particularly important to the purchaser. Similar patterns and shapes can be found with a maker's backstamp of "E Radford".

Woods' "Ringwood" ware has a bold formal backstamp. The "E Radford" mark is a freestyle facsimile signature, although the patterns on Radford ware seem to be largely more traditional in both colouring and style. The range of shapes produced by Woods was far more extensive than that by Radford.

"Piazza-ware" vase, 1950s, ht 22cm/8¾in, **£30–40/$50–65**

Italian 1950s

Italy has a long tradition of hand-decorated pottery, and many towns have their own style of decoration. "Maiolica" and other very textural hand-built pieces are typical of Italian output in the 1950s and 1960s. The clay does tend to chip quite easily, and the glazes can flake, but the decorative quality of the wares will often override these defects. Fine art was adapted into decorative techniques very quickly in Italy, and Jackson Pollock's style of "dribbling" paint was soon employed on vases, lamp bases and planters. Pablo Picasso also had a huge influence on Italian pottery, and aspects of his work seem to have been lifted directly onto ceramic designs. Piero Fornasetti, who updated the old to create exciting new patterns, is now considered to have been a major player in late 20thC design.

▼ Plate and jar by Piero Fornasetti

Piero Fornasetti (1913–88) took images of faces and buildings and added a witty touch by collaging on top of them. Astronomical and ex-catalogue illustrations, like the taps below, were combined with lettering or areas of gold lustre on bone china to make giftware. Lustres wear badly in use, and this can affect the price of these items.

Plate and jar by Piero Fornasetti, c.1960, plate diam. 25cm/10in, jar ht 19cm/7½in, **£75–100/ $120–160 (each)**

▶ Plaid-patterned bowl

This occasional fruit bowl would have been very cheap to buy when it was new. Italy exported huge numbers of similar pieces in infinitely different shapes and designs. Variations of checks or fruit and wine motifs were particularly popular. The glaze on many of these items is of poor quality, and can therefore chip very easily. If the pattern or shape of the piece is especially good then it is worth overlooking such damage, as long as it is reasonably minor.

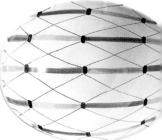

Plaid-patterned bowl, 1950s, diam. 21cm/ 8¼in, **£15–20/ $25–30**

FACT FILE

There are Italian ceramics at both ends of the price scale: Fornasetti and Fantoni pieces are auctioned for quite large sums, but many smaller factories produced pieces that do not command high prices as yet. A shrewd investment would be the 1950s hand-modelled and decorated "fancy" items – they look great, and display the spirit of their time.

▼ Lamp base by Fantoni and jug by Desimone

Picasso's own pottery was freely decorated, and Italian ceramicists employed a similar style of expression. Marcello Fantoni decorated on-glaze with bright enamel colours, having used *sgrafitto* or incising underglaze to add to the quality of the image. Similarly Picasso-influenced are Desimone's pieces. Flasks and bottle-shaped forms have trailing outline illustrations and Picasso-esque faces with colour infill. These are decorated on the glaze before firing so the colours spread and blur slightly.

Lamp base by Fantoni and jug by Desimone, late 1950s, lamp base ht 40cm/16in, jug ht 16cm/6¼in, **£60–90/$95–145 (each)**

Peasant pottery pair of Italian vases, 1960s, ht 10cm/4in, **£10–20/ $15–30 (each)**

▲ Peasant pottery pair of Italian vases

Many great pieces of Italian pottery have little to identify them. However, the Faenzarella Pottery in Vietri produced large quantities of stylish, textured ware that is easy to spot as it consists of rich, bright colours and a milky glaze over a greyish clay. Designs were changed on a regular basis in Italian pottery so a great variety of patterns and shapes was produced. Texture was often added, as well as spots and other shapes, to give added relief to the design.

▼ Matching pair of yellow-and-grey jug and vase

These items illustrate the daring shapes that the Italian potteries were making during the 1950s. The combination of yellow and grey was highly fashionable, and the black stripe pattern added an extra dimension. Although probably quite impractical, they would have made a bold statement in an interior. The extravagant shapes and the fact that there are two pieces together make these items very collectable.

Matching pair of yellow-and-grey jug and vase, 1950s, jug ht 29cm/ 11½in, vase ht 15cm/6in, **£75–90/$120–145 (the pair)**

Scandinavian

Sweden, Denmark and Norway became a huge design influence around the world in the 1950s and 1960s. "Swedish Modern" became a catchphrase for a style of interior that encompassed light woods, clean lines and up-to-the-minute styles. While much of Europe had been shut down creatively during the war years, Scandinavia had continued to develop. Wilhelm Kage and Stig Lindberg at the Gustavsberg factories were highly influential designers – Lindberg (1916–82) produced decorations that were copied all over Europe. Potteries like Uppsala-Ekeby produced arty pieces, while the Rorstrand and Gefle potteries made modern dinner and decorative wares, Marianne Westman's "Picknick" for Rorstrand being the most famous. The 1960s saw a move back to natural colours and less exaggerated shapes – practicality determined the form and restraint in the patterns.

Vase and dish by Stig Lindberg, early 1950s, vase ht 20cm/8in, **£90–120/$145–190**, dish diam. 23cm/9in, **£40–50/$65–80**

▶ **Vase and dish by Stig Lindberg**
The influence of Lindberg's work on 1950s ceramics cannot be overstated. He began to make his mark with elastic shapes and organic decoration. "Faience" painting (a tradition similar to maiolica) was revitalized with his stripes, figures and leaf patterns. Hourglass vases and curling leaf-form bowls are typical of his 1950s work. His designs are indicated by the distinctive hand print on the backstamp, above.

▼ **"Picknick" cheese board by Rorstrand**
Rorstrand was one of the main factories in Sweden to be committed to modern design. Marianne Westman designed for it under the direction of Gunnar Nylund. "Picknick", first produced in 1956, is probably the most famous and popular of Westman's designs. A print of stylized vegetables and herbs in black is brightly hand coloured and then matched with a deep red glaze on the lids. The shapes are functional and decorative, and are ideal for use in a 1950s-style kitchen as the pottery is very durable.

"Picknick" cheese board by Rorstrand, c.1956, 29cm x 27cm/11½in x 10¾in, **£50–75/$80–120**

"Fajance" covered box by
Royal Copenhagen,
ht 5.5cm/2¼in,
£35–50/$55–80

◄ **"Fajance" covered
box by Royal Copenhagen**
This charming box is part
of the extensive "Fajance"
range of pottery produced
throughout the 1960s by
Royal Copenhagen. The Danish
factory exported its generally
abstract artistic output widely.
The colours tend to be earthy
and natural on many of the
later decorative items, while
blues and purples dominate
the earlier range, as seen above.
Its "Marselis" range of vases
is also highly collectable. The
three wise men shown on this
box are decorated by hand over
a printed image; the blue-grey
colour in the background is
typical of the "Fajance" range.

FACT FILE

Most Scandinavian pieces
were fairly expensive
when new, and they
have retained their
value. Many of the
original owners still
value their Scandinavian
pottery far too highly
to part with it, so finding
the better pieces of Stig
Lindberg and Royal
Copenhagen can be
difficult for collectors.

"Saga" vase by
Figgioflint, 1960s,
ht 22.5cm/9in,
£25–30/$40–50

► **"Saga" vase
by Figgioflint**
Similar to Arabia,
the Figgioflint
and Stavangerflint
factories both
produced highly
decorative as
well as functional
ranges. Dinner-
ware patterns
like "Lotte" and
"Market" showed
figures at work
and play within
decorative borders.
The "Saga" pattern by
Figgioflint has a strong
Scandinavian feel – mythical
characters peer out from
the highly stylized foliage.
Decorated on elegant
earthenware shapes, the
transfer-printed design almost
smothers the whole area.
The backstamp very often
only has two "F"s and a
stylized water motif on it.

▼ **Black-and-white decanter
and ashtray by Arabia**
Manufactured in Finland,
these Arabia items show the
humour and popular touch
of illustration often found in
Scandinavian ceramics. The
decanter is modelled as a
figure, with the stopper in
the shape of a hat. The
decoration is incised, and
the detail kept to a minimum.
The ashtray is one of a range
of pieces, each with a fence
design as a border, and an
activity depicted in the
centre such as reading,
cooking, walking or
entertaining a baby,
as here – all in fine
line drawings. Spindly
plants often fill the
decorated areas of
the wares, but the
designs are never
overfilled or
spoilt by this.

Black-and-white decanter
and ashtray by Arabia,
1950s, decanter ht 20.5cm/
8¼in, **£80–100/$130–160**;
ashtray w. 13.5cm/5¼in,
£15–20/$25–30

Homemaker

When this pattern was first made for Woolworths in 1955 it was designed to appeal to the young who were setting up home for the first time, hence the name "Homemaker". It has since been put on a design pedestal. Style-aware couples would have seen the boomerang table, the Gordon Russell sideboard and Robin Day chair as symbols of youth. Enid Seeney's design used fashion icons of the day, but the pattern did not appear to become less popular as interior fashions changed, and pieces have been noted from as late as 1970. The textured pattern used as a background for these images was typical of textile designs of the time, many of which were science-inspired due to new technology such as electron microscopes; designers took images from them and created their patterns. This particular pattern was sold in Woolworths stores all over the world; a rare item is a rust-coloured version – these were produced for the export market.

▼ Milk jug

This milk jug would have been difficult to decorate with an all-over pattern, so cut-outs of the illustrations were taken to form the design. The large areas of white give this jug a different feel from the flatware pieces. As more collectors discover "Homemaker", rarer items like this jug are becoming harder to find, and prices are increasing. The rarest items in the flatware are the oval meat platters. Plates and cups and saucers would have been used every day, so were made in large quantities, but not all customers would have bought the larger pieces, which explains the rarity of those today.

Milk jug,
ht 12cm/4¾in,
£30–60/
$50–95

▶ Coffee-pot

The goal of every collector of "Homemaker" is to find the elusive tea and coffee pots in the pattern. In terms of availability, the coffee-pot shown here is the easiest to find, but even so some collectors look for years before they find one. The body is decorated in the same way as the milk jug. Specialist shops are the most likely place to find one of these. The "Cadenza"-shaped teapot is the rarest of all these items, and if this is ever spotted it simply must be purchased.

Coffee-pot,
ht 15.5cm/6¼in,
£100–200/
$160–320

"Homemaker" is an enduring collectable – new people are drawn to it all the time for its sense of nostalgia or fun. Though it was produced in huge quantities when originally sold, today there will always be a waiting list for the better items, so collectors must be patient.

Soup bowl, diam. 22.5cm/9in, **£40–60/$65–95**

▲ Soup bowl

Apart from the oval platters there are other items on the wish lists of many collectors, and the 1950s-style cereal bowls with their steep sides are particularly desirable. The rimmed soup bowl illustrated is also a particularly difficult shape to find – perhaps the modern pattern on such a traditional shape did not prove popular at the time. Smaller fruit dishes are not quite as rare, but are still certainly worth snapping up if they are on offer.

Vegetable dish (tureen), diam. 24cm/9½in, **£60–90/$95–145**

▲ Vegetable dish (tureen)

The ultra-modern look of this vegetable dish explains why it is among collectors' favourite items. These dishes traditionally had a handle on either side of the base, but to match the coupe (rimless) style of the plates the design was refined into this streamlined UFO-style shape. As these dishes were in the more expensive part of the range they are now quite sought after, and are far harder to find than the Homemaker flatware or cups and saucers.

Fantasia side plate by Burgess and Leigh, 1959, diam. 15cm/6in, **£15–20/$25–32**

▼ "Fantasia" side plate by Burgess and Leigh

This bold black-and-white design makes clever use of familiar kitchen objects, abstracted to create a look that is influenced by, but different from, the "Homemaker" pattern. First made in 1959, and designed by Harold Bennett, "Fantasia" was a stylish entry into contemporary style for Burgess and Leigh. Manchester City Museum and Art Gallery had a range of pieces remade for commercial sale in the 1990s. The pieces were boxed as gift items, and had modern backstamps to differentiate them from the originals. (The original body colour was slightly creamy, with black hollow-ware.)

MARKS

There are two stamps: a simple italic text "Homemaker, Made in England" and the more illustrative version below. Small dates are often noticeable on either side of the bases, and these can help to date shapes.

RIDGWAY POTTERIES LTD
HOMEMAKER
MADE IN STAFFORDSHIRE ENGLAND
ALL COLOURS GUARANTEED
UNDERGLAZE
AND DETERGENT PROOF

Polish, Czech & German

Modern design in the late 1940s had made its mark in Scandinavia and the USA, but much of Europe was too busy rebuilding after the war to indulge in the fashions of the day. The "New Look" emerged from Paris in 1947, and this exaggerated outline had slowly crept into everyday design in the rest of Europe by the early 1950s. Hourglass elegance was embraced by the ceramics and glass industries over the decade to supersede the hard lines of the pre-war Art Deco and Modernist era. Royal Dux and Cmielow produced extravagantly shaped bone-china tableware and ornaments from the beginning of the 1950s; Thomas and Rosenthal in Germany made high-fashion tableware throughout the late 1950s and early 1960s; and designer Raymond Loewy produced the classic service "2000" shape for Rosenthal in 1954.

◀ **Bone-china jug and sugar bowl by Cmielow**
The organic look of the 1950s was embraced by Cmielow – its teaware was so daring in shape that it had an almost "melted" appearance. Decoration was sparse, as it was the shape that made the bold statement of these designs, and *sgrafitto* lines worked by hand on the colour were therefore often the only adornment to the shapes. Pastel colours like pink and grey were mixed, and rich turquoises and glossy blacks were used to contrast with the bright white body colour.

Bone-china jug and sugar bowl by Cmielow, 1950s, jug ht 13.5cm/5¼in, sugar bowl ht 13cm/5in, **£20–30/ $32–50 (the pair)**

▼ **Animal and ashtray by Cmielow**
Decoration is similarly sparse on this figural deer and ashtray. Bold strokes of black or aerographed colour usually highlighted the features on birds and animals, and the eyes were sometimes worked in *sgrafitto*. Graphic black and white was fashionable for ornaments, which were often set against a bold-coloured background. Gold lustre is used on some of the more traditional Cmielow products.

Animal and ashtray by Cmielow, 1950s, animal ht 13cm/5in, ashtray diam. 13.5cm/5¼in, **£30–40/ $50–65**

Cruet by Goebel, 1960s,
vinegar bottle ht 7.5cm/3in,
£25–35/$40–55 (the set)

▲ Cruet by Goebel

These oil and vinegar bottles
and jam pot are decorated
with bold 1960s motifs.
Illustrations of bottles, pepper
mills and other domestic
items were used as a form
of fashionable decoration
on tableware and fancies
throughout the decade.
Novelty cruets and jam pots
were popular gift items and
could therefore afford to be
whimsical and kitsch. Though
bright and fashionable, these
textile-style prints are at the
more expensive end of the
market, and the artwork is
of very good quality.
Goebel produced a
number of variations on
these domestic patterns.

▼ West German black-and-colour vases

The West German potteries
mass-produced fashionable
hand-decorated ware in the
1950s and throughout the
1960s. These 1950s examples
were decorated with a resist
technique, and were hand
coloured and then finished with
black. Crescents, plaids and
multi-coloured stripes feature
on many of these pieces. They
are often only backstamped
with "Foreign" and little more,
which makes identification
extremely difficult. The ware
is very liable to flaking, but the
quality of the design usually
outweighs the minor flaws
that may be found on a piece.

West German black-and-colour vases, ht 15cm/6in,
£20–35/$32–55 (each)

▼ German houses-and-trees vase

This elegant German vase has
the trademark low handle and
thin neck of its mid-century
vintage. The stylized trees
and abstracted houses are
scattered over the ware.
A mixture of hand painting
and *sgrafitto* has been used,
and the limited colour range
adds to the style of the piece.
The base has
"handarbeit"
(hand crafted)
written on it. Such
anonymous pieces
can be excellent
examples of their
time, especially
as a collector will
not have to pay
designer-label
prices for them.

German houses-and-trees vase,
late 1950s,
ht 25cm/9¾in,
**£15–20/
$25–32**

Midwinter 1950s

W. R. Midwinter was founded in 1910 and quickly developed from a small family business into one of the larger potteries in Stoke-on-Trent before World War II. After the war Roy Midwinter, son of the founder, took over as design director. He was influenced by American west-coast potteries, and his "Stylecraft" shape, launched in 1953, broke the mould of traditional British ceramics. The "Fashion" shape of 1955 was even more extreme, and the use of in-house designer Jessie Tait, along with Hugh Casson and Terence Conran, gave the factory a lead over its competitors. Jessie Tait's name appeared on most of the decorative backstamps on the ware. Colin Melbourne produced figures in the modern style, and a range of fancies by Terence Conran, featuring bicycles and other forms of transport, is now extremely sought after.

▼ **Vase by Jessie Tait**

Vase by Jessie Tait, 1956, ht 17cm/6¾in, **£125–175/ $200–280**

The Midwinter Jessie Tait vases, candlesticks and flask-and-beaker sets were made from 1956, and were based on hand-thrown shapes that she had produced. Decorated with slip trailing or tube-lining in black, with contemporary-style textures or motifs, they are among the most popular Midwinter collectables. Banding in red and blue was also employed on some of the shapes, such as the lemonade sets, and these are of a higher value. The later pieces were decorated with stock transfers of roses or simply with plain glaze colours.

▶ **"Zambesi" tureen by Jessie Tait**

The shape known as "Fashion" was launched in 1955 with decorations by Terence Conran and Jessie Tait. Trends in interior design at this time had moved from textiles to wallpaper and ceramics, and Jessie Tait's 1953 "Homeweave" pattern was textile inspired, as is this bold hand-painted zebra-stripe pattern. "Zambesi" employed underglaze black stripes and on-glaze red enamel to create the brightest red available. Very popular with 1950s enthusiasts, the tea and coffee ware is increasingly sought after, and the tureen, or vegetable dish, illustrated here is a must-have from the range.

"Zambesi" tureen by Jessie Tait, 1956, ht 9cm/3½in, **£40–65/ $65–105**

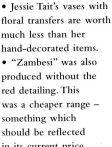

FACT FILE

• Jessie Tait's vases with floral transfers are worth much less than her hand-decorated items.
• "Zambesi" was also produced without the red detailing. This was a cheaper range – something which should be reflected in its current price.

"Chequers" plate, 1957, diam. 36cm/14in, **£30–50/$50–80**; "Nature Study" cup and saucer, 1955, diam. 15cm/6in, **£20–30/$32–50**

▲ "Chequers" plate and "Nature Study" cup and saucer

Terence Conran (b. 1931) produced only a handful of designs for the Midwinter factory in the 1950s, but they have all become favourites with collectors today. "Nature Study" was a striking design based on leaves and insects, drawn in a naive style on white flatware and twinned with satin-black glazed items. His last pattern, "Melody", reworked the rose motif.

▼ "Red Domino" cup and saucer by Jessie Tait

The "Red Domino" pattern on the cube-shaped "Stylecraft" range was a huge success when launched in 1953. Painted on-glaze in red, with hand-applied white spots, the pattern was in production well into the 1960s and was widely copied by many factories; the items most often confused with it are Kirkham's rolling pins and storage jars, but neither of these shapes was made by Midwinter. This pattern can suffer greatly in use, so check that the spots have not chipped off and that the red has not turned brown through overuse.

"Red Domino" cup and saucer, 1953, cup ht 6cm/2¼in, **£15–20/$25–32**

"Festival" teapot by Jessie Tait, ht 17cm/6¾in, **£100–200/$160–320**

▲ "Festival" teapot by Jessie Tait

Jessie Tait's "Festival" pattern paid homage to the 1951 Festival of Britain, though it was designed some years later. Science was an inspiration to many designers of the time, and the molecular image here, one of the first patterns to be launched on the futuristic "Fashion" shape, was hand-painted onto it. The flowing lines and high loop handles were inspired by Eva Zeisel's designs. The dinnerware is easier to locate than the tea and coffee ware.

MARKS

This is typical of the backstamps on 1950s Midwinter pieces. The pattern name is often positioned on top of the design, the date below it.

Midwinter 1960s

Staying one step ahead of its competitors, Midwinter launched the "Fine" shape in 1962. This collaboration with David Queensberry dictated British trends for the next decade. Early patterns like "Sienna" and "Queensberry" were instantly popular, and were emulated by all their competitors. "Mexicana" and "Piccadilly" continued the "stripe" designs. Further experiments in pottery shapes were not commercially successful, but they have become highly collectable owing to their comparative rarity. Psychedelic-inspired patterns like "Spanish Garden", "Eden" and "Alpine Blue" began the flower-power pottery craze in the later 1960s. In 1968 a take-over by J. & G. Meakin (see pp.48–9) rationalized the Midwinter shapes, and "MQ2" and "Portobello" were withdrawn from production. Decorations by freelance designer John Russell sold throughout the decade, although his commercial style is not as popular with collectors at the moment.

▼ "Diagonal" teapot by Nigel Wilde
Nigel Wilde worked for Midwinter as a freelance designer, producing three tableware designs. This pop art-inspired pattern was very difficult to make, as the slightest difference in the size of the clay item would have meant that the pattern did not fit the piece. Despite plates being sized to overcome this problem, the pattern was finally withdrawn, and has now become one of the most sought-after ones on the "Fine" shape.

"Diagonal" teapot by Nigel Wilde, 1964, ht 14cm/5½in, **£25–30/ $40–50**

"Riverside" teapot and "Oranges and Lemons" jug by John Russell, 1963, teapot ht 16.5cm/6½in, **£20–30/ $30–50**; jug ht 11cm/4¼in, **£4–5/$6–8**

▲ "Riverside" teapot and "Oranges and Lemons" jug by John Russell
John Russell's naturalistic fruit and floral images were a modern tableware option for those who did not want the more youth-orientated abstract designs. The colours were darker, like the green glaze used on the "Riverside" pattern. The "Oranges and Lemons" hollow-ware was light brown.

Although many of the patterns in production throughout the 1960s were made in huge quantities, there are still rarities: biscuit barrels and sugar sifters with chrome accessories were sold through limited outlets, and patterns like "Mediterranean" and "Diagonal" were only sold for a short period.

▼ "Spanish Garden" coffee-pot by Jessie Tait

This is probably the most popular pattern produced on tableware in the 1960s. Jessie Tait's "Spanish Garden" was originally inspired by a Liberty tie. The vaguely psychedelic pattern and colours appealed to a broad market, and it sold through to the late 1970s. Produced on the revised flat-lidded teaware in the "Fine" range, it is still in use in many British homes today.

"Spanish Garden" coffee-pot by Jessie Tait, 1966, ht 20cm/8in, £18–30/$32–50

"Sienna" soup bowl and saucer by Jessie Tait, 1962, bowl diam. 15cm/6in, saucer diam. 16.25cm/6¼in, £10–12/$15–20

▲ "Sienna" soup bowl and saucer by Jessie Tait

"Sienna" and "Queensberry" were the most influential patterns on the new cylindrical teaware of the early 1960s. Lug or solid handles took the place of open handles on soup bowls and gravy boats. Adding to this modern look was the contemporary stripe decoration in a muted, natural-colour palette. Although these Jessie Tait pieces are today mostly sought by dinnerware-matching companies, they also have an increasing collector's market.

▼ "Pierrot" teapot by Nigel Wilde

Nigel Wilde produced this quirky Paisley-esque pattern on the ill-fated "MQ2" shape in 1967. Transfer-decorated in blue on a white body, this "Pierrot" pattern utilized the limitations of the shape by decorating all the areas that would accept a transfer motif. Based on a chemist's bottle, the idea was carried through to the other shapes in the range. However, the problems with the shape were never resolved, and it was eventually withdrawn from production in 1968 when J. & G. Meakin took over the factory.

This backstamp was used from 1962 to the mid-1970s. Older backstamps that utilized the distinctive shapes of the plates were also used in the 1960s.

Midwinter
FINE   TABLEWARE
STAFFORDSHIRE ENGLAND
SHAPES DESIGNED BY THE
MARQUIS OF QUEENSBERRY

"Pierrot" teapot by Nigel Wilde, 1967, ht 15cm/6in, £30–40/$50–65

Poole Pottery

Poole Pottery, formerly known as Carter, Stabler & Adams, has always had an artistic and creative output as a commercial pottery. In each decade the pottery has produced innovative pieces that have become classics in their field. Delicate florals were made from the 1920s through to the 1960s. Soft pastel colours were mixed with a speckled grey glaze to form the popular "Twintone" patterns of the 1930s and these were sold in the 1960s and 1970s. Embracing the 1950s look, a range of vases called "Freeform" was produced, which are now among the most valuable pieces Poole made. Pieces from the "Delphis" range are today sold as artwork, as the painters and paintresses initialled their work. Tony Morris and Guy Sydenham were major forces at Poole from the early 1960s, and have their own collector-following as well.

▼ **"Freeform" vases by Alfred Read**

These classic vases were made from 1954 as part of the "Freeform" range. Alfred Read designed the patterns, and worked with Guy Sydenham to produce the slip-cast and thrown shapes. Contemporary tableware patterns were produced simultaneously – these are much easier to find than the elusive larger vases. The complexity of the pattern affects the price: the vases pictured are at the higher end of the range; simple patterns and traditional shapes are more plentiful and cheaper to buy.

▶ **"Delphis" plate**

This range is far too broad to cover here with the depth it deserves. The early "Studio" range of "Delphis" pieces dates from 1964, although one-off "Studio" pieces were made from 1961. Most Delphis pieces do not have the word "Studio" on the backstamps, but some have the signature or monogram of the decorator. This can affect the price a great deal, as some were "top names" while others were local art college students. The "Delphis" colour range was reduced in 1971 to red, orange, yellow and green with a black keyline; the range was discontinued in 1980.

"Delphis" plate, c.1964, diam. 12.5cm/ 5in, **£30–40/ $50–65**

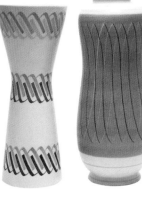

"Freeform" vases by Alfred Read, left 1956, right 1954, ht 30cm/12in, **£300–500/ $480–800 (each)**

Floral bowl and plate by John Adams, bowl diam. 20cm/7¾in, **£10–15/$15–25**; plate diam. 15cm/ 6in, **£8–20/$13–32**

▲ Floral bowl and plate by John Adams

Simple but stylish hand-painted florals had formed a popular Poole range since the 1930s. Some patterns were recoloured or adapted to suit modern trends, as coupe (rimless) plates were a style requirement for the design-conscious in the 1950s. Mainly worked in pastel and soft, natural colours, these pieces are great examples of the quality of hand painting that has been maintained at Poole Pottery. Fruit motifs like the apple pattern "Pippin", abstracted leaf patterns and flowers are sometimes mixed with mushroom, jade or turquoise hollow-ware.

Prawn serving dish by Robert Jefferson, 1962, diam. 38.5cm/15¼in, **£12–15/$20–25**

▲ Prawn serving dish by Robert Jefferson

Robert Jefferson took over as resident designer at Poole in 1958, having graduated from the Royal College of Art in London. He brought a new approach and new technology with him. The advancement of printing processes meant a better-quality image in reproduction, and he exploited this. His 1962 "Lucullus" collection of oven-to-tableware included this charming dish. A one-colour print with matching glaze colour was lightened by a stroke of light red applied by hand to each prawn.

▼ Twintone cruet & trefoil dish

The speckled grey "seagull" glaze was matched with a range of plain colours for tableware and some decorative pieces. Turquoise and greens, as here, were the most popular colours, but a deep red-brown and a lime green were also used. The shape of this cruet is very distinctive, as with the other cruet items that Poole produced. This particular design is most probably by John Adams.

Cruet & trefoil dish, 1950s, cruet ht 8.5cm/3¼in, **£15–20/$25–32**; trefoil dish diam. 26.5cm/10½in, **£18–25/$30–40**

Bjorn Wiinblad

Bjorn Wiinblad began working with pottery in his native Denmark in the middle of the 20thC, and has since produced an incredible range of designs. His distinctive style is instantly recognizable and is becoming increasingly collectable. Wiinblad's earlier drawings and paintings were inspired by his environment and by folk tales – elves and sprites populate his woodland scenery – and his early pieces for the Nymolle factory also feature bold portraits, or tell a story. He produced a selection of modelled items, usually figural, and some studio pieces that are highly collectable because of their limited numbers. His output for the German factory, Rosenthal, includes illustrated series and dated plates, delicate porcelain fancies and relief patterns. He also designed the shapes for ranges of teaware with simple banded decorations.

Rosenthal vase, 1960s,
ht 26.5cm/10½in,
£40–75/$65–120

▶ **Rosenthal vase**
This tall cylindrical vase is part of the "Flora" range. It was produced by Rosenthal in the 1960s, but the body colour is stained to match the Nymolle "look". The drawing probably symbolizes the goddess Flora, and the same style of vase was available in various sizes. Cylindrical shapes are prone to hairline or body cracks – a gentle tap with your nail should produce a clear sound, but if the vase is damaged the tap will result in a dull thud.

▼ **Nymolle pendant**
This tiny pendant produced at the Danish pottery Nymolle is decorated with one of Bjorn Wiinblad's distinctive drawings. The quality of reproduction and detail are superb. It is part of a set of 12: each pendant has a month written on the back, so they could be given as birthday presents. Very often the "month" series of designs tells a visual story on each one. These pendants are likely to be quite difficult to find today.

Nymolle pendant, 1960s,
diam. 4.5cm/1¾in,
£20–30/$32–50

Wiinblad's work for Nymolle is easily spotted by the body colour and the illustrations in pink, blue, green, brown or black. The many pieces he did for Rosenthal are less easy to spot as they cover a huge range of styles, shapes and deco-ration, such as subtle relief patterns with carved scenes and gold lustre.

▼ Nymolle cat wall plaque

This wall plaque is richly detailed – the lady featured has a hat decorated with flowers and a cat in her arms, while another cat runs past in the background. Every area of the busy design is highly decorative. The foliage and check patterns are familiar Wiinblad trademarks. The softened square shape of the plaque is typical of Scandinavian design of the period.

Nymolle cat wall plaque, 1960s, diam. 19cm/7½in, **£25–35/$40–55**

Covered ceramic box, 1950s, ht 9cm/3½in, **£25–30/$40–50**

▲ Covered ceramic box

This bon-bon or pin dish is decorated in a pattern called "Opraline 1", worked in the traditional Nymolle black print on a tinted grey earthenware body. An all-over design is worked on the base, with stars and circles forming a net pattern. The illustration on the lid is typical Wiinblad exotica: a woman with extra-vagantly decorated hair is kneeling to feed an equally exotic bird some sweets from an open box. Foliage and abstract pattern complete the composition and add to the charm of the drawing. Nymolle covered boxes in a collection are a nice complement to plaques and other pieces that are intended for wall hanging.

Candlestick, late 1960s, ht 30cm/ 12in, **£350–400/$560–640**

▲ Candlestick

In the late 1960s and into the 1970s Wiinblad moved away from mass-production to return to a more hand-crafted approach to his pottery. This extravagant figurative piece has the Wiinblad sense of humour and distinctive pattern but is part of that move away from commercialism. An alternative to this Delft-like blue-and-white horse and rider is a centaur decorated with incised patterns.

Raymond Peynet

Born in France in 1908, Raymond Peynet began his career in advertising, and his distinctive and popular illustration style soon enabled him to start his own agency in Paris. His most enduring creation is a couple known as "The Lovers" – a man in a bowler hat and his elegant Parisienne partner. The almost surreal images he produced of this couple in endless scenarios eventually found their way onto ceramics. In 1952 Rosenthal approached Peynet to produce some designs; this collaboration was very successful, and many new pottery designs were created over the subsequent ten years. Peynet's work is also found on items made by the Danish company Nymolle. Peynet is now particularly popular in Japan, and the company Yamaka produced ceramics in 1994 decorated with his work. Sadly, Raymond Peynet died in 1999.

▼ Rosenthal lidded dish
This lidded dish opens to reveal a surprise inside. These images are typical of Peynet's style – especially the use of fine linework and pastel colours. A number of designs were produced for similar shapes; in one of these a gentleman is looking through a window on the lid, and inside his chérie is just leaving a bathtub, holding a small towel to save her modesty. These gift items were probably intended to be used as cigarette boxes.

Rosenthal lidded dish, 1960s, box and lid w. 14cm/5½in, **£40–50/ $65–80**

▶ Nymolle red-on-grey mermaid dish
This dish by Nymolle was first made in 1955, and is one of only eight designs by Peynet for the factory that were put into production. The mermaid is charming and illustrates the innocence and subtlety of Peynet's work. Images of mermaids, birds, park benches, trees and stylized music are recurring motifs on Peynet's pottery designs. It is thought that the eight designs produced for Nymolle were based on existing drawings rather than being specially commissioned original work.

Nymolle red-on-grey mermaid dish, c.1955, diam. 12.5cm/5in, **£15–20/ $25–32**

Peynet's distinctive style was utilized on posters, books, fabrics and even dolls. All of these are avidly collected, but the ceramic figures made in the late 1950s are the most sought-after pieces and therefore can be very expensive. Look out for repairs on pieces with modelling, as this can make a great difference to their value.

Nymolle "Lovers" plate, c.1955, diam. 14cm/5½in, **£25–30/$40–50**

▲ Nymolle "Lovers" plate

The couple on this plate are known as "The Lovers" and probably represent Peynet and his wife, Denise. Cupids and heart motifs were used in many of Peynet's designs, as were park scenes and musical references. The grey background or "body colour" is a trademark of the Nymolle factory. The same print also appears in black on some pieces. Peynet's images are funny, poignant and sometimes genuinely sad. The direct style and familiarity of the characters make each piece appealing, and because Peynet's drawings were so widely used in the 1950s and 1960s, on posters and in magazines, his ceramics were popular gift items. Nymolle employed many artists for its ranges of fancy items, so a facsimile signature was often included on the backstamp.

▼ Rosenthal porcelain figures

Peynet's wispy and delicate drawings translate incredibly well into three-dimensional figurines and tableaux. Designed from about 1957 to 1960, a range of ornaments, candelabra and novelties was modelled and produced by the German company Rosenthal. The modelling was so detailed that little decoration was needed to capture the Peynet style – on this model the man is reading music from his partner's garters. Soft colour has been added to the trimming on her dress and headwear, and the definition on his jacket, hat and trousers completes the piece.

Rosenthal porcelain figures, c.1958, ht 20cm/8in, **£150–400/$240–640**

Rosenthal calendar dishes, 1960s, diam. 9cm/3½in, **£20–24/ $32–40 (each)**

▲ Rosenthal calendar dishes

Plates and fancies with the months of the year were a popular Continental gift item. The bold colour on these small dishes is unusual for Peynet's work for Rosenthal. The images are reversed out of the colour, and perhaps because of this are less detailed. Finding the complete set of dishes will offer quite a challenge to the collector, as Peynet's work is increasing in popularity nowadays.

Portmeirion

Susan Williams-Ellis and her husband, Euan, took over Grays Pottery (as it was then called) in 1960. Susan began to design original and striking coffee and tableware items, and gold lustre features heavily on her early work. Black and white engravings of Victorian imagery then became the vogue in the mid-1960s, and Susan produced an innovative decoration with her "Totem" design which, combined with her "Cylinder" range of shapes, made the factory as famous as the village the pottery was named after. Storage jars with Greek-key decorations were a very successful line for Portmeirion and made their way into most homes of the day. The black-and-white images were updated towards the end of the 1960s; placed on bright psychedelic mugs and fancies they were perfect for the younger generation. Susan continued to design best-selling patterns – the most well-known is probably the "Botanic Garden" pattern, from 1972, which is still in production.

◀ "Dolphin" spice jar
The "Dolphin" design was originally made solely for Portmeirion village souvenirs, but was later sold through Grays Pottery, and by other stockists from 1960. The original finish had a pink lustre background or a mix-and-match collection of Neapolitan colours. Having proved its sales potential, "Dolphin" was extended from herb, spice and larger jars to include rolling pins, jugs and plates. The bright colours used on these pieces make them appealing today, though the black-and-white pieces made in the late 1960s are likely to be the most plentiful.

"Dolphin" spice jar, c.1962, ht 8.5cm/3⅜in, **£18–30/ $30–50**

▼ "Tivoli" coffee-pot
This design on the "Serif" shape of 1964 was based on the Tivoli Gardens in Copenhagen; much of Susan Williams-Ellis' inspiration for shapes and patterns came from her travels. This all-over screen-print decoration was intended to be cut to fit any cylindrical shape. However, the design is prone to damage on the lids, and on the rims of the cups, which will obviously affect the value of a piece.

"Tivoli" coffee-pot, 1964, ht 30.5cm/12¼in, **£30–45/$50–70**

"Totem" jug

From its launch in 1963, "Totem" took the pottery market by storm. Portmeirion, being a relatively small manufacturer, could not cope with the huge orders that were received. Rival companies soon produced their own versions, but none had the imaginative decorations of the original design. The colours vary a great deal in the "Totem" range – there are light-blue, pewter and pale-green versions that were all commercial successes.

"Totem" jug, 1963, ht 12.5cm/5in, **£15–20/$25–30**

Black-and-white tankard by Susan Williams-Ellis, 1960s, ht 10.75cm/4¼in, "Zodiac" tankard by John Cuffley, 1969, ht 10cm/4in, **£5–15/$8–25 (each)**

▲ Black-and-white tankard by Susan Williams-Ellis & "Zodiac" tankard by John Cuffley

Portmeirion discovered copper-plate engravings from the 19thC and early 20thC when it bought Kirkham in 1962 (see p.58). Susan dusted them down and placed them on all manner of shapes – many of them were from bizarre patent medicines or "veterinary ointments". John Cuffley's 1969 "Zodiac" range was placed on white, black and coloured mugs and plates.

see p.58

▼ "Velocipedes" terracotta tankard

A tongue-in-cheek sense of humour was often found on Portmeirion's decorative transfer decorations. The "Velocipedes" series was inspired by an article in the *Strand* magazine, and unlikely names and captions were added to this collection of early bicycle designs. Eve Midwinter, who worked for Portmeirion for a brief period in the late 1960s, did some of the illustrations.

"Velocipedes" terracotta tankard, late 1960s, ht 12.25cm/4¾in, **£15–20/$25–32**

Rye Pottery

The small family-run pottery in Rye was founded in 1947 by two brothers, Walter and John Cole, when they took over the Bellvue Pottery that had closed before World War II. A pottery tradition already existed in this Sussex coastal village, and there was a wealth of talent and expertise to be tapped. Making slipware-decorated items, the Coles managed to work around the post-war Utility restrictions. A distinctive style was formed with the use of tin glazes and maiolica decoration, and the pottery still uses the same methods of production today. Hand-thrown and slip-cast pieces were decorated with stars, dots, stripes and *sgrafitto*, and these all make Rye Pottery items easy to spot today. Despite the size of the pottery the company managed to sell all over the country, as well as overseas.

▼ **Small vase**
by David Sharp
David Sharp (b. 1932) joined Rye pottery in 1947 straight from Maidstone College of Art as an apprentice. He worked at Rye, decorating and throwing, until 1956 and his work from this period has an impressed "D" on it, making it easy to recognize. Sharp then left to work at Cinque Ports Pottery before forming his own company, David Sharp Pottery, in the early 1960s. His highly distinctive decorated figures of animals are widely recognized by collectors. This small vase is freely decorated, and not typical of the Rye style; many of his other pieces have far simpler decoration.

Small vase by David Sharp, 1947–56, ht 8cm/3¼in, **£40–50/ $65–80**

Pair of miniatures by John and Walter Cole, 1950s, diam. 4cm/1½in, **£30–35/$50–55 (each)**

▶ **Pair of miniatures**
by John (1908–98) and
Walter (b. 1913) Cole
The Bellvue pottery had had a history of making miniature pieces, and this tradition continued after the Cole brothers took over, and throughout the 1950s. These pieces are often too small to bear any backstamp but are decorated in the distinctive Rye manner, using the soft primary colours and spiral patterns that were commonly used on coasters, plates and other wares produced at Rye Pottery during the 1950s and 1960s.

▼ Four "Cottage Stripe" miniatures by John and Walter Cole

This "Cottage Stripe" pattern, which can be seen on a number of hand-thrown and cast shapes, is one of the success stories at Rye, and has been in production almost continuously since 1947. Variations on the pattern were produced, including dots and simpler stripes, and the designs were given evocative names such as "Candy" and "Fairground". Early pieces of the pattern were made in a red clay. This can be seen on the base of the piece, which often also bears an impressed mark for the pottery. The later backstamp simply says "Made in Rye, England".

Four "Cottage Stripe" miniatures by John and Walter Cole, 1950s onwards, red jug ht 11.5cm/4.5in, **£10–£80/$15–130 (each, depending on size or rarity)**

▶ "Lambeth" squares-and-stars tankard by John and Walter Cole

The "Lambeth" pattern was inspired by an early English piece of maiolica ware from Lambeth Pottery. Tankards for beer or hot drinks were popular Rye items, and there are many varieties of shape and style to be found. A nice added extra is the small piece of clay that was placed on top of the handle to be used as a thumb grip. Most tankards were hand-thrown with an applied handle, often with a characterful swirl at the base. Extra details, such as the ribbed base on this piece, were sometimes added to the body.

"Lambeth" squares-and-stars tankard by John and Walter Cole, early 1950s, ht 10.5cm/4¼in, **£25–35/$40–55**

Hornsea

Hornsea Pottery was founded by two brothers, Colin and Desmond Rawson, in the north of England in 1949. They gradually built the business up to a 64-strong work force by 1954, producing small giftware items such as Toby jugs. John Clappison had been at art college in nearby Hull before attending the Royal College of Art, London. He produced designs for Hornsea in his summer holidays, extending the repertoire of styles at the factory. The pottery moved towards good, modern design from this point, and his work put the factory on the map. Ranges of naturalistic animal figures in tree stumps or logs were the mainstream output through the late 1950s and early 1960s. Towards the end of the 1960s, mass-production and the popularity of dinnerware saw the decline of the more hands-on designs, though innovation was always an ingredient in any Hornsea range.

Fish light by John Clappison, 1961–3, ht 24.5cm/9¾in, **£200–300/$320–480**

▶ **Fish light by John Clappison**
In the early 1960s, when this impressive light was made, it retailed at about £2.25 ($3.60). It was not produced in large numbers, and this fact, combined with the fragile extremities of the fish, makes it quite a rare item. The large fish is hand-decorated with sponging on the body; the small fish light is in relief and is left undecorated. This quintessential John Clappison design is keenly sought by Hornsea collectors today.

▼ **"Rainbow" planter**
The "Rainbow" pattern, with its distinctive ridges, was hugely successful between 1961 and 1963. The hand decoration meant that no two pieces were the same, and the blue-and-yellow colourway is as appealing to the modern market as it was when it was first produced. The planters were available in different sizes, and cruets, vases and other functional shapes were also decorated with these unusually bright colours.

"Rainbow" planter, 1961–3, ht 14cm/5½in, **£20–30/$32–50**

"Sunflower" planter, 1965, ht 14cm/5½in, **£18–25/$30–40**

▲ "Sunflower" planter

Planters are ideal collectables as they always maintain their usefulness around the home, no matter how old they are. This "Sunflower" design dates from 1965, and the piece illustrated is one of a set of three pots, which were decorated using stencils. These planters were available in five different colourways. The blue-and-green version shown above is the one most commonly found today.

"Tricorn" bowl, 1958, diam. 16cm/6¼in, **£25–40/$40–65**

▲ "Tricorn" bowl

This distinctly 1950s pattern, which is called "Tricorn", is based on triangular forms and dates from 1958. Produced on a wide range of shapes, the graphic turquoise and black colours are striking against the white body colour. Star, or "sputnik", motifs on each of the sides add to the period feel of the range. Cruets, vases, ashtrays and this bowl are among the variety of shapes that were made. These pieces are all fairly difficult to find now, especially in good condition, as the range was not a success at the time.

Studiocraft "Thorn" vase, c.1960, diam. 13.5cm/5¼in, **£30–40/$50–65**

▲ Studiocraft "Thorn" vase by John Clappison

The Studiocraft logo was added to the backstamp of some ranges from 1960 to 1962 – usually the most fashionable designs, such as "Home Décor". John Clappison modelled the dozen or more pieces in the range with relief spikes or dots and finished them with a matt creamy-white glaze. These pieces are very fragile, and the most minor damage can put collectors off. Now selling in larger auction houses, they may be tomorrow's big collectables.

J. & G. Meakin

J. & G. Meakin was a well-established family-run Stoke-on-Trent pottery during the 1950s. Although it made attempts at the fashionable side of tableware at this time, it was not until 1964, with the launch of the "Studio" shape by the industrial designer Tom Arnold, that it succeeded. The tall cylindrical form of the coffee-pot followed the lines of Portmeirion's "Cylinder" shape (see p.42) and David Queensberry's "Fine" range for Midwinter (see p.34). Tall and slender, with a chunky easy-to-grip lid and up-to-the-minute graphics, this shape was produced in a huge variety of patterns to meet public demand. Collectors have already seized on the coffee-pots as major collectables, and a row of differently patterned pots of the same shape makes a great collection. J. & G. Meakin became part of the Wedgwood group in 1970.

▼ **Polka-dot "Domino" teapot**

This "Domino" teapot was likely to have been following the trend for spot patterns led by two companies, T. G. Green and Midwinter. Instead of a blue or red version, J. & G. Meakin produced this stylish decoration on earthenware, with printed black spots on the body of the teapot and a sleek glossy black lid. The matching tableware in softened square shapes was decorated with the printed spot pattern. Although currently less collectable than its contemporaries, this distinctive shape is sure soon to be as sought after as Midwinter's "Red Domino" design.

Polka-dot "Domino" teapot, 1950s, ht 15cm/6in, **£30–40/ $50–65**

▶ **"Manderley" coffee pot by Jessie Tait**

In 1968 J. & G. Meakin took over the Midwinter factory. The latter had overstretched itself with an innovative new shape, "MQ2", designed by Roy Midwinter and David Queensberry (see p.35). When Meakin took over it discontinued this shape, and the transfers and designs were adapted for use on its "Studio" range. As a result of the take-over Meakin gained Midwinter's top designer, Jessie Tait. "Manderley" was one of her designs. Originally intended to be placed on the "MQ2" range, it actually seems ideal on this coffee-pot.

"Manderley" coffee pot by Jessie Tait, c.1969, ht 20cm/8in, **£12–15/ $20–25 (£35–45/ $55–70 for coffee set for six people)**

"Impact" plate by Jessie Tait, 1969, diam. 18cm/7in, **£3–5/$5–8**

▲ "Impact" plate by Jessie Tait

This Jessie Tait design was produced specifically for the "Studio" shape range of pieces. "Impact" uses the colourway that was particularly popular at the time – blue and green were fashionable interior colours. The bold circles mixed with foliage showed the influence of pop art. The design of "Studio" plates had moved away from the coupe (rimless) style of the 1950s and now had a gentle raised edge to prevent spills.

▼ "Aztec" tureen

This was one of the most popular 1960s dinnerware patterns that was made on the "Studio" shape. Turquoise-coloured glazed lids picked out the colour in the transfer motifs. These textured motifs, which are reminiscent of stained glass or a mosaic, showed the influence that ancient cultures had on the company's designs. Other potteries also had a similar idea – for example, the "Totem" pattern produced by Portmeirion (see pp.42–3). Dinnerware is generally less popular with collectors as it is more difficult to display.

"Aztec" tureen, diam. 22cm/8¾in, **£10–15/$15–25**

Meakin's "Studio" range is, at the moment, very much an affordable collectable. The coffee-pots have been collected for some time, as they display well and have such graphic patterns. The flatware is also good display material, as there tends to be a border pattern and central motif on each of the pieces.

▼ "Inca" jug and sugar bowl by Jessie Tait

The distinctive square handle on the jug shown below echoes the coffee-pot shape from the same set. This Jessie Tait design was very popular and sold well into the 1970s. The geometric pattern looks like a mixture between a scientific cross-section and an architectural detail. The orange-and-brown colourway became de rigueur in the 1970s, when there was a distinctive move away from the bright psychedelic colours of the late 1960s.

"Inca" jug and sugar bowl by Jessie Tait, c.1970, jug ht 9cm/3½in, bowl ht 7cm/2¾in, **£4–6/$7–10 (the pair)**

This backstamp appeared on almost all of the "Studio" range pieces throughout the time that the shape was in production.

Troika

The Troika Pottery was formed in St Ives, Cornwall, in 1963. Troika initially produced small decorative items but graduated to larger sculptural pieces as it became better known and expanded its staff and capacity. By 1964 the factory was producing items for the top London stores Liberty and Heal's. In the early days of the factory the production was both textured ware and the less distinctive white glaze-finished items. The influence of the Cornish landscape – tin mines and the rugged coastline – can be seen in both the shapes and the decoration of Troika's wares. The influence of painters like Paul Klee has also been cited as inspiration. The factory moved to Newlyn in 1970 and, despite its continuing successes through the decade, closed in 1983. Following a major exhibition in 1994 Troika has become widely collected – larger pieces are now sold through London auction houses, and examples are represented in museums.

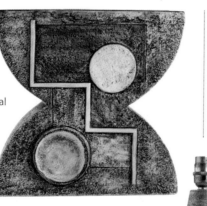

"Anvil" vase, 1960s,
ht 22cm/8¾in,
£250–350/
$400–560

▶ **"Anvil" vase**
This striking sculptural piece is known as "Anvil" and was probably intended to be ornamental rather than practical. The colour range used on Troika pottery is quite muted, and the use of blue in particular is generally quite limited. Because the artists at Troika were not trained as potters they experimented with daring shapes such as the one shown here. This is also one of the most collectable pieces for the same reason.

▼ **Lamp base**
Troika always trod a fine line between creating saleable pottery and maintaining its artistic integrity. The wares were displayed in the pottery's shop. Troika found that giving items a practical use, such as this lamp base, meant that the public were less hesitant to buy the pieces. The square and cylindrical forms Troika used lent themselves to being made into lamp bases without commercializing the output too much.

Lamp base, 1960s,
ht 36cm/14½in,
£150–200/$240–320

Tapered "Coffin" vase, 1960s, ht 17.5cm/7in, **£45–70/$70–110**

▲ Tapered "Coffin" vase

This small vase and Troika's cube-shaped ornaments and jam pots represent the typical smaller pieces that the pottery produced. Most of these are easily available to the collector today. The quality of decoration affects the price: a clean graphic image or a popular symbol like the Egyptian "Ankh" will probably be more expensive than a piece with minimal decoration.

▼ Large sculptural vase

This large vase is among the most expensive pieces of Troika available, and illustrates the "Troika look" perfectly. The vase is very architectural and reveals the influence of Ancient Egypt and monoliths, buildings and temples from earlier cultures. The textured quality is crisp, and the pattern is worked on different layers. The colour is applied quite freely but the palette is limited, and the resulting surface imitates stone and slate. Stylized figures, faces and other images can be seen in the larger Troika pieces, while the cylindrical items are largely geometric.

Large sculptural vase, 1960s, ht 36cm/14½in, **£350–450/ $560–720**

Floral-motif plate, 1960s, diam. 29cm/11½in, **£90–120/$145–190**

▲ Floral-motif plate

This plate is much less distinctive than all the other pieces shown here, but it does have a hand-painted Troika mark, as well as that of the potter, impressed in the base. Unlike the bulk of the factory output, which was mould-made, this plate has been hand-thrown. Floral motifs in the same style as the one shown here were often combined with the whiteware (untextured) designs.

Carltonware

The Carltonware factory started life at the end of the 19thC as Wiltshaw and Robinson – the recognizable Carltonware script backstamp did not appear until the mid-1920s. Rich lustred decorative vases and ginger jars were produced at this time. The highly distinctive textured leaves and flowers on fancy shapes appeared in the early 1930s and continued well into the 1950s. Quirky and characterful shapes always featured heavily in the factory's output. During the 1950s, as modern design dictated new trends, softer shapes and simpler colours began to prevail. Two-colour patterns took the place of ornate multi-coloured designs. Then, as the 1960s "look" developed, abstract transfer prints and a more natural colour palette were used on its decorative pieces – browns and greens were particularly popular with Carltonware.

▲ "Hazelnut" cruet
This pattern, and a similar design called "Convolvulus", were used to illustrate the simpler shapes produced by Carltonware during the 1950s. "Hazelnut" was available in two different colourways, and the cruet pieces stood on a dark-green base. The brown-and-cream colourway is less popular with collectors at the moment, but this is sure to change as the pieces become harder to find. However, tea-pots in either colourway are always extremely sought after.

"Hazelnut" cruet, 1950s, ht 5cm/2in, **£45–55/ $70–90 (the set)**

▼ "Windswept" cheese dish
This pattern is probably the best example of "organic modernism" in British tableware from the 1950s. All the lines are fluid, the handle is integral, and the decoration is simple and does not fight against the shape. Available in two shades of green or brown and made on a wide range of shapes, the motif is transfer-printed. "Windswept" does not normally command the prices of the more decorative patterns; this is probably because its simplicity does not appeal as much to Carltonware collectors.

"Windswept" cheese dish, 1950s, diam. 23.5cm/9¼in, **£15–22/ $25–35**

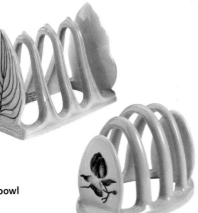

Condition is paramount with Carltonware. As many of the pieces were produced in huge quantities, damaged items are worth considerably less than perfect examples. Badly restored pieces are also often found on the open market, so if the price is low check the piece over carefully. Check toastracks in particular for damage or repair, as they are very fragile by nature.

▼ "Leaf Salad" bowl and servers

Part of the "Leaf Salad" range from the late 1950s, the servers shown here are in the rust-and-cream colourway, and the bowl is in two shades of green. A lime-green version and a two-tone grey were also popular at the time. The butter dish in the range is particularly attractive. The exuberant shapes and imaginative forms of these designs are typically 1950s. Ceramic salad servers are obviously prone to damage, and are very often repaired, but most other shapes in the range should be easily found with little or no damage.

"Leaf Salad" bowl and servers, late 1950s, bowl ht 12cm/4¾in, **£30–50/$50–80**; servers l. 19.5cm/7¾in, **£25–35/$40–55**

Toastracks, late 1950s, "Pinstripe" (tan) l. 11.75cm/4½in, "Magnolia" (green) l. 13cm/5¼in, **£45–65/$70–105 (each)**

▲ Toastracks

Toastracks were a popular gift item, and many factories specialized in producing imaginative and unusual varieties. Carltonware produced functional and decorative toastracks in most of its patterns. "Pinstripe" is another leaf-form design from the late 1950s and was produced in a number of colourways, including rust and a fresh, bright green. "Magnolia" was produced at about the same time.

▼ Vegetable cruet

Mainly produced in the 1960s, this cruet is part of the "Fruit" range, which included tea and coffee ware based on apples and pears. This vegetable cruet, modelled as a celery leaf with peas, carrots and onions, was very popular, and is still high on collectors' lists. However, finding all the pieces in pristine condition is becoming quite difficult.

Vegetable cruet, 1960s, diam. 22.5cm/9in, **£60–80/$95–130 (the set)**

Denby Pottery

The Denby factory was founded by the Bourne family in the early 19thC and produced salt-glazed and utilitarian wares for the greater part of its first century. From the 1880s to the 1920s its output was more like that of Doulton, and the influence of the Art and Crafts movement was very apparent in its work. Glyn Colledge and his father, Albert, produced distinctive hand-painted decoration during the 1940s and 1950s. Glyn Colledge's leaf patterns appeared on dinnerware and vases, and his abstract designs can be found on the elusive "Cheviot" range. Tibor Reich, probably better known at the time for his textile designs, worked on a freelance basis for Denby in the 1950s, and his shapes and patterns, though uncharacteristic for Denby, are keenly hunted down by collectors.

Tankard by Glyn Colledge, early 1950s, ht 13.5cm/5¼in, **£25–30/$40–50**

▶ **Tankard by Glyn Colledge**
"Glyn-Ware" was produced from the late 1940s and is typically found with stylized leaf patterns swirling over the ware. This tankard probably dates from the early 1950s, though the styles of body and handle vary a great deal and can be difficult to date. The pieces were very often worked in dark greens and earthy browns; some have details in bright turquoise, acid yellow and red. Vases with similar designs in broader brushstrokes are part of the "Glyndebourne" pattern, dating from about 1960.

▼ **"Arabesque" plate by Gill Pemberton**
This classic 1964 pattern, by Denby designer Gill Pemberton, was inspired by a visit to Russia. Ochre and red details were hand painted onto a rich dark-brown glaze. The most popular item from this design is the coffee-pot, and its waisted shape is carried through to the cruet and other hollow items. This pattern was produced on a huge range of shapes, and is popular today with both collectors and those still using the service. "Arabesque" was withdrawn in 1984.

"Arabesque" plate by Gill Pemberton, 1964, diam. 25.5cm/10in, **£6–12/$10–20**

This scroll backstamp is found on some items of "Green Wheat", though a special backstamp was designed for the pattern. Later pieces may have other generic marks.

▼ "Tigo-Ware" by Tibor Reich

"Tigo-Ware" was a new direction for Denby. Stark black-and-white designs were worked on an earthenware body (most Denby pieces were stoneware). A striking label marked the base of the pieces and incorporated Reich's name. "Tigo-Ware" was not in production for long as it was slow and labour-intensive. Some of the elaborate pieces are almost impossible to find today, though the simpler bowls and stripe patterns were made in larger quantities.

Tigo-Ware by Tibor Reich, c.1956, coffee-pot ht 27.5cm/11in, **£25–300/ $40–480 (each)**

▼ "Green Wheat" platter by Albert Colledge

This rectangular meat or serving platter is an Albert Colledge design and was first produced in 1955. The oven-to-table quality of the stoneware body was a major factor in its popularity. The design was entirely hand painted by a team of paintresses, and it remained in production until 1976. This was a popular export design, selling to the USA, Australia and New Zealand. The pattern appears on a variety of shapes and the hollow-ware items have a rich dark-green glazed interior.

"Green Wheat" platter by Albert Colledge, 1955, w. 34cm/13¼in **£28–35/$45–55**

• Patterns like the mix-and-match coloured "Galaware" were aimed at the US market, and are unlikely to be found in any great quantity in the UK.
• Kenneth Clarke, a designer for Denby, produced some designs for vases and table-ware in the 1950s contemporary style, including "Cotswold" and "Asphodel" (both ranges of footed and asymmetric vases).

Broadhurst & Kathie Winkle

A clever move by many factories in the 1950s and 1960s was to put their designers' names on the backstamp of the wares. This raised the profile of the company and made it seem design-conscious and modern. Broadhurst followed this trend by adding the name of its in-house designer, Kathie Winkle, from about 1964. Many collectors were not sure if this was a real name, but a brief biography on her work has now been published. This has drawn attention to the factory and increased interest in her work. Born in 1932, Winkle joined Broadhurst in 1950 and produced her first design for the factory, "Pedro", in 1958. As a designer she worked well within the constraints of the decorating process; many patterns are simple borders, but she also created all-over patterns. The prolific Broadhurst output included "Rushstone", which sold in excess of 50 million pieces.

▼ "Calypso" and "Bermuda" plates
These plates illustrate the Broadhurst method of decoration. Simple images are stamped on the biscuit ware and are then hand coloured and glazed. Leaves were a perennial image used on all decorative interior accessories throughout the post-war period, through to the 1960s. The "Calypso" pattern, with its scattered leaves, was highlighted with swiftly applied strokes of colour, while the "Bermuda" design required more detailed work.

"Calypso" and "Bermuda" plates, c.1960, diam. 24cm/9½in, **£4–6/ $6–10 (each)**

▶ "Tyne" tea trio
This attractive tea trio dates from about 1961 and is a mixture of hand painting and "stamped" designs. The style of decoration is typical of the designs produced by Broadhurst at the time. The influence of block-printed textiles can be seen, as the pattern would work equally well as a fabric design. The ware was sold as inexpensive and up-to-the-minute fashionable – few patterns of this period were in production for any great length of time. Many of the patterns have coloured cups, which increased production and brought down costs.

"Tyne" tea trio, c.1961, plate diam. 16.5cm/6½in, **£12–15/ $20–25 (the set)**

There is little difference in the price of Broadhurst and Kathie Winkle signed pieces at the moment, but new Kathie Winkle patterns are still being unearthed, and collectors are adding to their knowledge. Once a core of collectors has been established, rarer items will become sought after and prices will inevitably start to rise.

• Writing the factory or designer name at an angle had been popular since the 1930s, and Broadhurst continued the tradition. A simpler oval backstamp was also used.
• Kathie Winkle was given credit as designer on the back of her designs from 1964, though, rather cheekily, the factory also used her name on some patterns that she had not designed.

▼ "Capri" bowl and "Corinth" tea plate by Kathie Winkle

When a Malkin "stamping" machine was used an image could be transferred onto plates and bowls with speed, and a paintress could then add the coloured details to lift the design. As this had to be worked quickly, the paintress was paid by the number of pieces finished, and the detail colour was applied boldly, adding to the lively quality of the designs. For this reason many of the designs are quite simple border patterns.

"Capri" bowl and "Corinth" tea plate by Kathie Winkle, 1960s, bowl diam. 15.5cm/6in, **£1–2/$2–3**; plate diam. 17cm/6¾in, **£2–3/$3–5**

"Electra" coffee-pot by Kathie Winkle, 1969, ht 21.75cm/8½in, **£15–20/$25–30**

▲ "Electra" coffee-pot by Kathie Winkle

This distinctive coffee-pot is part of the "Delta/Riviera" range of shapes, and was cleverly designed to enable machine decoration on the outermost band. Once the black design was printed, colour was added by hand. The "Electra" pattern, first produced in 1969, shows a strong Art Nouveau influence. Tea and coffee pots, along with serving items like gravy boats and stands, are some of the more difficult Broadhurst items for collectors to find.

Kitsch homestyle

Having been deprived of decoration and colour for a number of years, post-war Britain went mad with its decorative schemes in the early 1950s. In an average living room, one wall might be papered with a decorative abstract design, while the other walls could be painted red, turquoise, pink or yellow. The carpet and upholstery would also usually be patterned. Among this colourful setting nestled vases, plant pots and figurines. Interior accessories were also the theme on tableware designs and "Homemaker" was a prime example of this (see pp.28–9). Cutlery, lighting and plant-pot designs adorned teapots and plates. However, in the 1960s there was a backlash against this movement, and during that decade classic and tasteful restraint became the order of the day.

◀ **"Spots and Stripes" jug by Kirkham**
This simple but popular range was made by the Kirkham Pottery, Stoke-on-Trent, and is found on a wide variety of shapes, including sifters, plates and preserve pots. Metal and teak holders were sold with butter dishes and other lidded items. The inspiration for the pattern may have come from Jessie Tait's "Magic Moments" design. Some pieces have a rubber-stamped date, but there are quite a few examples with no backstamp details, and these may have been made by a different company. There are also plates carrying the Portmeirion mark, dating from after the take-over in 1962.

"Spots and Stripes" jug by Kirkham, 1959–62, ht 13cm/5¼in, **£12–15/ $20–25**

▶ **Chef-and-stripe jug and sifter by Kirkham**
This lively pattern was made between 1959 and 1962. Kirkham was then taken over by Portmeirion Pottery, which continued to make its designs for existing customers (see pp.42–3). The Portmeirion backstamp appears on some pieces. The naive stick-man on this jug and sifter has a chef's hat and is dancing with plates of food. This mad imagery is completed with "cocktail stick" lettering naming every piece "bowl", "sifter" and so on. The use of striking yellow and red was perfect for the modern kitchen of the time, and is equally popular with many collectors today.

Chef-and-stripe jug and sifter by Kirkham, 1959–62, ht 11cm/4¼in, jug, **£15–20/ $25–32;** sifter **£20–30/ $32–50**

Flying ducks by Keele, 1950s, w. left to right 14.5cm/5¾in, 16.5cm/6½in and 18.5cm/7¼in, **£75–200/$120–320 (set of three)**

As a rule, the more wild a pattern was at the time of manufacture the more quickly it dated, and therefore the easier it is to spot as a symbol of its day. The flying ducks, though restrained in decoration, were decidedly 1950s, and the exuberant tableware, with cacti, cutlery and chefs, could not belong to any other era.

▼ Soup cup and plate by Crown Ducal

Many traditional and long-established factories dipped their toes in the water and tried to compete with the "modern" look. Crown Ducal produced this wild transfer design of potted plants and leaves within a piece of patio furniture. Although the shapes are still traditional, the lively image and red detailing were designed to tempt younger buyers. It also updated its tubelined designs from the 1930s and 1940s. These were in a palette of red, grey and black on satin-white glaze.

Soup cup and plate by Crown Ducal, 1950s, cup diam. 11cm/4¼in, plate diam. 16cm/6¼in, **£10–12/$15–20**

▲ Flying ducks by Keele

Many such charming birds flew across the chimney breasts and hallways of British homes from the 1950s onwards. The varieties are endless: sometimes there were four or five, or they were seagulls or even more exotic bird life. Many factories in Stoke had their own "breed" of duck, and other potteries around the country joined in the fun and made their own distinctive versions. Cheaper versions were made in chalk or plaster, and have not usually survived in very good condition. Many of the sets have had countless repairs, so condition is therefore quite important and should be reflected in the price.

▼ "Long-line" cutlery teapot by Bristol

Cutlery had appeared on all surfaces as a decorative motif during the 1950s. This strong graphic use of engraved images is reminiscent of Fornasetti (see p.24). Produced by the Bristol Pottery, the "Long-line" range of kitchenware was an alternative to dull utilitarian kitchen pots. The range was functional as well as decorative and won *Good Housekeeping* magazine's seal of approval. The range's kitchen storage jars sported bright primary-colour lids.

"Long-line" cutlery teapot by Bristol, 1950s, ht 8.5cm/3½in, **£20–35/$32–55**

Glossary

Backstamp The factory identification mark on the base of a piece of pottery; this can be painted or printed; if a paintress worked on an item she would add her mark to the base, as she would be paid for the number of items she had finished each day; this method was known as piecework

Dinnerware-matching companies Companies that supply out-of-production ceramics to people who are still collecting old services

Fancy items Pieces with no definite function; ornaments, decorative dishes and bowls or vases were termed fancy items, as they were luxury items rather than necessities in the way that plates were

Hand painting A design completely worked by hand; Midwinter and Poole produced some entirely hand-painted designs; many companies printed images that were then hand coloured

Hand coloured This was a faster method of production that allowed a more accurate finished result; the printed image could be tinted to add detail, or given a wash of colour to highlight areas

Hollow-ware Plates, saucers and shallow bowls are referred to as "flatware", whereas open shapes like cups, vases and teapots are hollow and therefore termed "hollow-ware"

Impressed mark A factory mark was sometimes stamped into the wet clay to leave a self-coloured identification mark; most Wedgwood pieces have this mark, and occasionally the date the piece was made as well

Lustre Metallic oxides used to create gold, silver or other rich effects on pottery

Maiolica The technique of painting a design onto the glaze before it is fired, to allow the colour to diffuse through the glaze as it is firing

On-glaze enamel Some colours (red, for example) are very difficult to achieve under the glaze as they can burn away during the firing; an on-glaze enamel colour could be painted over the glaze and then fired; gold, platinum and copper lustres are all applied on-glaze

Open-stock transfer printing Companies sold many patterns to more than one pottery and this helped to reduce the cost of commissioning a design and producing large amounts of transfers that might not be needed; open-stock transfers are also used today

Resist A technique in which a pattern is masked off and the colour or glaze is then applied to the rest of the item to create a different effect for that area

Seconds Finished objects that were not up to standard or had minor flaws were sold as seconds; very often these are indistinguishable from the best-quality items unless the backstamp has been scratched through or marked with "second quality"

Sgrafitto Before clay has been fired it is possible to scribe decoration into the item with a stylus (sharp pen) or *sgrafitto* tool; this method of decoration can also be used on porcelain and bone china where a colour is sprayed onto the blank pottery; the design can then be etched out of the colour – drawing in negative

Slip Clay in its wet form, when it contains enough water to flow freely

Slipware Pottery items are dipped into a tinted or coloured mixture of clay and water to give them an even colour before being decorated; Cornish ware, for example, is decorated using this method

Stamping For speed, some potteries use rubber stamps with simple images to decorate their ceramics; this can be either in a colour on the biscuit or unglazed item, or in a lustre on a glost, or glazed, piece; most of Broadhurst's ware utilizes stamped images

Stencil Many potteries use stencils to speed production of a pattern; the image is cut out of card or metal and the colour sprayed through onto the clay; this is much faster than hand painting and also gives more uniform results

Transfer An image can be printed onto a film that burns away during firing to leave the image bonded to the pottery item; transfers are then applied on top of the glaze

Tube-lining Clay slip is tinted with colour and then applied to the unfired clay to create outlines or designs; the artist

Jessie Tait used this method on her series of vases for Midwinter (see p.32)

Underglaze Decorating under the glaze gives a more durable result, so this term describes designs that were applied to the pottery before it was fired

What to read

Atterbury, Paul
Cornish Ware
(Richard Dennis, UK, 1996)

Atterbury, Paul and Hayward, Lesley
Poole Pottery
(Richard Dennis, UK, 1998)

Atterbury, Paul and Hayward, Lesley
Poole Pottery in the 1950s
(Richard Dennis, UK, 1997)

Atterbury, Paul, Denker, Ellen Paul & Batkin, Maureen
Twentieth-Century Ceramics
(Miller's, Mitchell Beazley, UK, 1999)

Austerity to Affluence – British Art and Design 1945–62
(Merrell Holberton Publishers with The Fine Art Society/Rayner & Chamberlain, UK, 1997)

Hopwood, Irene and Gordon
Denby Pottery 1809–1997
(Richard Dennis, UK, 1997)

Jackson, Lesley
The New Look Design in the '50s
(Thames and Hudson, UK, 1991)

Jenkins, Steven
Midwinter Pottery –
A Revolution in British Tableware
(Richard Dennis, UK, 1997)

Jenkins, Steven and McKay, Stephen P.
Portmeirion Pottery
(Richard Dennis, UK, 2000)

Leath, Peter
The Designs of Kathie Winkle
(Richard Dennis, UK, 1999)

Marsh, Madeleine
Miller's Collecting the 1950s
(Miller's, Mitchell Beazley, UK, 1997)

Marsh, Madeleine
Miller's Collecting the 1960s
(Miller's, Mitchell Beazley, UK, 1999)

Where to see & buy

Most city museums have ceramics displays and larger cities have dedicated displays of 20thC decorative arts – in Britain the Victoria & Albert Museum, London, and Manchester City Art Gallery are particularly good. Exhibitions or temporary displays highlighting the work of a period, pottery or designer are often advertised in the press or local library. New specialists shops open regularly, but these tend to be within bigger cities such as London or New York. Fortunately many antiques centres are aware of the interest in 20thC ceramics and now stock a broader range than they did five or ten years ago. Markets can be good hunting grounds, although the 20thC stock is variable. It is also worth looking out for specialist dealers.

ANTIQUES MARKETS AND SPECIALIST DEALERS

Alfie's Antique Market
13–25 Church Street
London NW8 8DT
(Various dealers specialising in 20thC decorative arts)

John Bostock
020 8878 5750
(Scandinavian specialist)

Camden Passage
Adrian Grater
The Georgian Village
Camden Passage
London N1 8EA
(Wed/Sat; 20thC Ceramics)

Camden Town
Unit H33, The Old Horse Hospital
The Stables, Chalk Farm Road
London NW1 8AH
020 8341 4897
(Sat/Sun; 20thC decorative arts)

Covent Garden Jubilee Market
London WC2E 8BE (Mondays)

Richard Dennis Gallery
144 Kensington Church Street
London W8 4BN
020 7727 2061
(20thC and contemporary decorative arts)

Festival
124 South Ealing Road
London W5 4QJ
020 8840 9333
(Midwinter and Portmeirion)

Flying Duck Enterprises
320–322 Creek Road
London SE10 9SW
020 8858 1964
(Decorative arts and kitsch)

Freeforms
Unit 6, 58–60 Kensington
Church Street, London W8 4DB
(Scandinavian and British 20thC ceramics)

Gary Grant – Choice Pieces
18 Arlington Way
London EC1R 1UY

020 7713 1122
(20thC ceramics gallery)

The Ginnel Gallery
18-22 Lloyd Street
Manchester M2 5WA
0161 833 9037
(20thC decorative arts)

Luna
23 George Street
Nottingham NG1 3BH
0115 9243267
(Selection of 20thC ceramics)

Rupert D'oyly
Stall 16
141–149 Admiral Vernon
Arcade, Portobello Road
London W11 2DY
020 8743 6741
(Sat; 20thC decorative arts)

Target Gallery
7 Windmill Street
London W1P 1HF
020 7636 6295
(Modernist design post-1945)

Index

ACKNOWLEDGMENTS

Grateful thanks to all who loaned items and searched in their attics for these treasures: Karen and Gary Boller, Stephen Walker, Nick Jenkins, Anne Wilkinson and Mike Crabtree, Harvey Ferry and Willie Clegg (The Country Seat), Jane Glennie, Phil Colechin, Martyn Palmer and Mark Jones, Ian and Anne Strover, Adrian Grater, John Bostock, Fig Taylor. Thanks also to Richard Dennis and Phillips Auctioneers and Valuers.

All pictures by Steve Tanner for Octopus Publishing Group Ltd, courtesy of Steven Jenkins, with the exception of:
7t OPG/Ian Booth/Zambesi; 8br OPG/Ian Booth/Rennies; 10l OPG/Ian Booth/Alfie's, 10r Racoon's Tale, Mullica Hill, NJ (USA)/Bert Denker; 11bl OPG/Tim Ridley/Deco Inspired; 12r Richard Dennis; 14t OPG/Robin Saker/Design Goes Pop; 18br OPG/Robin Saker/Ginnels; 21bl OPG/Tim Ridley/Madeleine Marsh; 24l & 24c OPG/Ian Booth/Alfie's, 25bl OPG/Ian Booth/Christie's South Kensington, 25bc OPG/Robin Saker/Ginnels; 26t OPG/Ian Booth/Christie's South Kensington; 29br OPG/Tim Ridley/Flying Duck Enterprises; 31tl OPG/Tim Ridley/Zambesi/Stables Market; 33tl OPG/Tim Ridley/Neil Bingham, 33tc OPG/Ian Booth/Alfie's, 33bc OPG/Robin Saker/Ginnels; 36bl OPG/Ian Booth/Alfie's; 39r Phillips Auctioneers; 41bc OPG/Robin Saker/Richard Dennis, 41r OPG/Robin Saker/Richard Dennis; 55b Richard Dennis